REVIVING
THE
BLESSED
HOPE
OF
THESSALONIANS
THE RAPTURE COMMENTARY SERIES VOLUME 1

Other Works by the Authors

Co-authored books by Stauffer/Ray:

Daily Strength 1—Devotions for Bible Believing Study (**2014, 455 pages, ISBN: 978-1-942452-17-1**)

Daily Strength 2—Devotions for Bible Believing Study (**2015, 439 pages, ISBN: 978-1-942452-27-0**)

By Andrew B. Ray:

The Fingerprint of God (**2011, 153 pages, ISBN: 978-1-602082717**)

By Douglas D. Stauffer:

One Book One Authority—2,000 Years of Church and Bible History (**2012, 888 pages, ISBN: 978-0-967701-60-8**)

One Book Stands Alone—The Key to Believing the Bible (**2001, 434 pages, ISBN: 978-0-9677016-7-7**)

One Book Rightly Divided—The Key to Understanding the Bible (**2006, 276 pages, ISBN: 978-0-967701-61-5**)

Freedom's Ring—Life, Liberty and the Pursuit of Salvation (**2008, 400 pages, ISBN: 978-0-967701-69-1**)

The DaVinci CON—The Great Deception (**2006, 128 pages**)

The Chronicles of Narnia—Wholesome Entertainment or Gateway to Paganism? (**2006, 236 pages**)

Other books, DVDs and CDs on eschatology:

Will the Church Go Through the Tribulation? (**2013, 144 pages**)

After the Rapture: Be Not Ignorant Brethren (**11 CD set, 12+ hours, UPC: 6-89076-67751-6**)

Changed by the Book—Learn to Study the Bible God's Way (**7 DVD set, 7+ hours, UPC: 6-89076-44624-2**)

In the Last Days (**4 DVD set, 434 minutes, UPC: 6-89076-677615**)

God's Wrath versus the Pre-tribulation Rapture (**3 DVD set, 384 minutes, UPC: 6-89076-67741-7**)

REVIVING

THE

BLESSED

HOPE

OF

THESSALONIANS

THE RAPTURE COMMENTARY SERIES VOLUME 1

DOUGLAS D. STAUFFER

ANDREW B. RAY

Copyright © 2016
McCowen Mills Publishers & LTB Publications
All rights reserved
Printed in the United States of America
Text Design: Rick Quatro (Carmen Publishing Inc., Hilton, NY)
Jacket Design: Chris Taylor (SeraphimChris, Pahrump, NV)

ISBN 978-1-9424520-2-7

Scripture quotations from the King James Bible need no permission to quote, print, preach, or teach. For clarity, all scripture is in italics with reference and any emphasis in bold print. Any deviation from the King James Bible is not intentional.

For more information, contact:
McCowen Mills Publishers
Dr. Douglas D. Stauffer, President
5709 North Broadway Street
Knoxville, TN 37918
(866) 344-1611 (toll free)
Website: *www.BibleDoug.com*
Email: *Doug@BibleDoug.com*

LTB Publications
Dr. Andrew B. Ray, Pastor
5709 North Broadway Street
Knoxville, TN 37918
(865) 688-0780 (Antioch Baptist Church)
Website: *www.LearntheBible.org*
Email: *pastorray@LearntheBible.org*

Dedication

This volume is affectionately dedicated to our faithful wives (Judy and Lula) and children (Justin, Ashley and Heather; Noah, Hannah, Sara, Charity, and Isaac). Thank you for your encouragement and understanding as God tasked us to write yet another book together. No man will ever complete the work of God so the sacrifice continues. Our prayer is that you will be richly rewarded in this life and eternally rewarded in the life to come. We could never do the work without the faithful support of each and every one of you!

"...but as his part is that goeth down to the battle, so shall his part be that tarrieth by the stuff: they shall part alike" **(1 Samuel 30:24b).**

We would also like to expand this dedication to those who truly want to know the truth of scripture. Without lovers of truth, there would be no need to write any Bible-based books. A special thank you toward those who have charged, and encouraged, and strengthened us though your prayers, input, and support. God knows who you are and so do we!

"But the hour cometh, and now is, when the true worshippers shall worship the Father in spirit and in truth: for the Father seeketh such to worship him. God is a Spirit: and they that worship him must worship him in spirit and in truth" **(John 4:23-24).**

Contents

List of Illustrations

Authors' Preface

Prophecy books and conferences far too often veil the underlying doctrinal beliefs of the authors or speakers until such time as the readers or attendees are either confused or deviously converted. This is quite alarming! The Bible should never be used as a means of trickery, deception, or suppression of truth. The authors of this work consider integrity most important necessitating a forthrightness concerning their positions and practices. We are unwilling to hide behind a mask or façade until such point as we have you convinced of our position or further confused. Furthermore, we make no apology for our doctrinal positions, nor do we believe that any scripture contradicts our writing (otherwise we would not have boldly proclaimed it).

Here are a few points concerning the authors' beliefs:

- We believe in the Blessed Hope which consists of a personal, premillennial, imminent return of the Lord for His body, the Church. Trusting in this Hope, according to scripture, has a direct significant bearing on one's personal life and holiness.
- We believe literal interpretation takes precedence when the Bible indicates a literal application and meaning.
- We believe the future holds this general sequence of events: the Rapture of believers, Daniel's Seventieth Week, the Second Coming, the Millennial reign of Christ, completion of the First Resurrection, followed by a New Heaven and earth.
- We believe and align ourselves with the futurist position (versus the preterist[1] or historicist[2] positions). The futurist teaches that many of the prophecies are yet to be fulfilled in the future, and in some

---

[1] The **Preterist** teaches that many of the prophetic teachings have already occurred in the past, especially a first century fulfillment concerning the most biblical texts. The **Partial Preterist** teaches that most prophecies in Revelation found fulfillment during the first century. The "thousand years" generally spans from that time up until the Second Coming and final judgment, thus often applying an allegorical interpretation. A **Full Preterist** teaches that all prophecies of Revelation have been fulfilled in the First century, including the Second Coming and the final judgment. Many of these teachers also teach that the Eternal State applies to this present time.

[2] The **Historicist** interprets the text as currently being fulfilled during the span of Christian History. The biblical text is sometimes taken as symbolic of real events, rather than being literally true.

cases might have an imminent fulfillment concerning the literal text; we believe in real physical events with an emphasis upon biblical literalism. A time of unprecedented tribulation precedes Christ's Second Coming. ***Daniel 9:27*** gives the seven-year chronological framework while Revelation chapters 6-18 offer the detailed judgments to come.

The authors of this work consider integrity most important necessitating a forthrightness concerning their positions and practices. We are unwilling to hide behind a mask or façade until such point as we have you convinced of our position or further confused.

- We believe that scriptural context (immediate, wider, and complete) takes precedence over all those factors of Bible study, interpretation, and *exegesis* (which simply means "exposition or explanation").[3] *Exegesis* is a part of hermeneutics (the science of interpretation). Paul gives us the primary command concerning Bible study and interpretation in *2 Timothy 2:15* which tells us what to do (study) and how to do it:

*2 Timothy 2:15 **Study** to shew thyself approved unto God, a workman that needeth not to be ashamed, **rightly dividing** the word of truth.*

---

[3] ***Eisegesis*** is the opposite approach of sound interpretation (the exegesis of scripture). Eisegesis involves someone reading his own thoughts or opinions into the text. It is very important to avoid coming to the Bible with preconceived notions, sometimes placed in the mind by those who mean well. Much can be said for the unlearning that needs to take place amongst those with indoctrinated concepts frequently caused by seminary educations. Furthermore, it is not the lexicons or Strong's Concordance that determine the meanings of παρουσία (parousia—presence, a coming, arrival or advent), ἐπιφάνεια (epiphaneia—appearing, manifestation, glorious display), and ἀποκάλυψις (apokálypsis—revelation, unveiling). Much of the lexical uncertainties used by those who consider themselves schooled in the original languages involve stretched and private interpretations. When the Bible gets subjected to private interpretation, those most guilty are usually the most educated with the best of intentions sometimes thinking that the ends justify the means.

- We do *not* believe the Pre-tribulation Rapture instigates any type of complacency amongst any serious Bible student. Quite the contrary!
- We do *not* believe that the Church was meant to live in comfort or ease during any period of history. Quite the contrary!

Our two-fold advice to the reader:

- **Live** every day as though this could be the day of the Lord's return. This expectancy leads to godly living because today could be the day when you see your Saviour face-to-face. This emphasizes evangelization in the short term.
- **Plan** as though you will be here for many more years to come. This leads to a long term spiritual and physical preparation for potentially difficult tribulations that the Church most likely will face. This emphasizes world missions over the long term.

> **Live** every day as though this could be the day of the Lord's return.
>
> **Plan** as though you will be here for many more years to come.

Any and all calls for **unity** must be based upon truth, not resulting from some misplaced fear of man, compromise of truth or tolerance for error. Tolerance for error eventually promotes heresy. Heresy always causes confusion. Confusion concerning the truth is never from God.

*1 Corinthians 14:33 For **God is not the author of confusion**, but of peace, as in all churches of the saints.*

Acknowledgements

The authors would like to express their deepest appreciation to the following:

Most preeminently, the precious Lord Jesus Christ for His saving and sustaining grace.

Those who invested the time and effort into our spiritual development, along with the men and women who have been persecuted and sometimes put to death for the faith and their trust in the Saviour and His word.

Our devoted wives for their constant support, encouragement, and understanding through our years of marriage and ministry together. They are truly God's *second* greatest gift to each of us *(Romans 6:23)*.

Mrs. Lois Barnes for her many hours of proofreading and grammatical suggestions.

Dr. Jerry Rockwell for his input reflected in appendix #5 and Mr. John Wright for his input after reading the manuscript.

Mr. Rick Quatro and Mr. Jonathan Judy for their invaluable assistance in formatting the book text.

Mr. Chris Taylor for his creativity reflected in an impressive cover design.

Lastly, the members of Antioch Baptist Church, Knoxville, TN for their faithful support and encouragement during this process of writing another book while faithfully serving with them.

Extended Author Biographies

Dr. **Douglas D. Stauffer** is an internationally recognized authority in the fields of Bible history, apologetics, and prophecy. He is a prolific author, having written over a dozen books along with writings published in Christian periodicals. Because of his biblical expertise, *Oxford University Press* commissioned Dr. Stauffer to work as one of two contributing editors for the notes on the *New Pilgrim* King James study Bible.

Immediately, following high school, Doug served a four year tour of duty in the USAF. Upon discharge, he returned to Pennsylvania to attend *The Pennsylvania State University,* graduating with a BS degree in accounting. A few months later he began attending Bible college.

While attending Bible college, Dr. Stauffer passed the CPA exam. He then worked as controller of several organizations. In 1994, he gave up his work as CFO of a multimillion dollar company along with managing his own firm when God began dealing with him about dedicating his time more fully to the ministry. Since that time, he has earned his ThM and then his PhD in Religion from *International Baptist Seminary*.

Along with being a frequent guest speaker on radio and television, he has served ten years in the pastorate and logged thousands of hours teaching in churches and at the college level. Dr. Stauffer currently serves as an evangelist and president of *Partners for Truth Ministries*. Doug and his wife Judy are blessed with two children, Justin and Heather.

Dr. **Andrew B. Ray** is the pastor of Antioch Baptist Church in Knoxville, Tennessee. He has a heart for the Lord, His word, the church, the family, as well as the next generation. He spends countless hours counseling and obediently declaring *"all the counsel of God."* As a diligent student of the scriptures, he earned his Doctor of Theology degree and faithfully preaches and teaches at the church, as well as the Bible institute.

Before becoming pastor in May 2007, Dr. Ray served as assistant pastor for four years at Antioch Baptist Church under Dr. David F. Reagan. Upon Dr. Reagan's death, Andrew was unanimously voted as pastor of Antioch Baptist Church.

Bro. Ray is the author of *The Fingerprint of God* along with a four year series of devotional books called *Daily Strength: Devotions for Bible-Believing Study*. He has also written several gospel tracts and is currently serving as an editor for a songbook that incorporates scriptural songs, bringing back original lyrics altered or removed by modern hymnals. He is truly what the Bible defines as a man who labours in the word and doctrine *(1 Timothy 5:17)*.

God has blessed Bro. Ray and his wife Lula with five children: Noah, Hannah, Sara, Charity, and Isaac. Introduction to the Book

Introduction to the Book

The Philadelphian Church Age basked in the sunlight of hope that is the Blessed Hope *(Titus 2:13)*. As the Rapture message flourished, it inflamed a desire within the saints of God to live holy lives and win the lost to Christ. During this period, revivals were widespread, souls were saved, hymns birthed, and churches planted. As the Blessed Hope mutated from a sure hope, the clarity and conviction of the Philadelphian Church Age gave way to the darkness of doubt, despair, and uncertainty found in the present Laodicean Church Age.

End-times' understanding has become much like the vision described by the prophet Isaiah *(Isaiah 29:9-14)*. Those who should be in the know are in a *"deep sleep"* having closed their eyes *(Isaiah 29:10; Revelation 3:17)*. Neither the *learned (Isaiah 29:11)* nor the *unlearned (Isaiah 29:12)* appear to offer definitive solutions concerning true Bible interpretation. Even those who believe and love the Bible seem to promote the Rapture by citing verses that neither speak directly of the Church's Rapture *(Revelation 4:1)* nor reference a Rapture at all *(Matthew 24:31)*. Additionally, those who trust in the ever allusive *"original autographs,"* that they neither possess nor any longer exist, cannot discern the difference between Israel and the Church, the Kingdom and the Church, or the Rapture and the Second Advent.

> Even those who believe and love the Bible seem to promote the Rapture by citing verses that neither speak directly of the Church's Rapture *(Revelation 4:1)* nor reference a Rapture at all *(Matthew 24:31)*.

The Bible frequently characterizes the Christian life as a battle and an athletic contest requiring discipline and endurance for success. Yet, many Christians are both AWOL and unfit for the spiritual challenge. Compounding the problem are those who expound the scriptures to others. Today's teachers are clouded by assumptions, presuppositions, and pet perceptions. Often, they simply continue teaching what they have previously taught or parrot what they have heard from their favorite teaching personality. This takes place without regard for the actual truth. Unfortunately, some of the most insidious attacks against truth have originated amongst those closest to the truth. This generally ensues because of pride, ignorance or personal ambition.

A return to the light of God's WORDS *(Psalm 119:130)* remains the only remedy for putting the darkness of doubt and despair to flight. No book, however well it may be written, will restore your hope in the Blessed Hope. No preacher, regardless of how charismatic, eloquent, or intellectual he may present himself, can clear the fog caused by false information concerning the end-times. You read that correctly! The authors of this work are not the authority. Not even close! The words

> No book, however well it may be written, will restore your hope in the Blessed Hope.

penned and typed are insufficient to restore anyone's lost hope. However, the SCRIPTURE contained within this work framed within their intended contexts can serve to restore the light and hope undermined through decades of inconsistent ambiguity.

After spending months reading, writing and researching, we are more convinced today of the Pre-millennial, Pre-tribulation Rapture than when we embarked on this spiritual endeavour. During the process of writing this commentary, our understanding has grown exponentially as students of Bible prophecy. We have become increasingly convinced of the soundness of our positions based upon Bible study, along with some sound exegetical and theological persuasions involving the brethren. This interaction has included brethren both aligned with Pre-tribulation Rapture eschatology and those adamantly oppose to this position.

We encourage you to trust the scripture! We invite you to evaluate our words in light of the perfect words of God! Where we may have erred, choose the Bible. However, we are convinced that anyone subservient to the scriptures will agree that the doctrine of the Pre-tribulation Rapture is the doctrine taught by scripture. This will not come to pass if we wrest the scriptures in order to cause them to prove an unprovable treatise, but only because this work explores the topic of the Pre-tribulation Rapture through the eyes of a contextual scriptural Bible study.

2 Peter 1:20 Knowing this first, that no prophecy of the scripture is of any private interpretation.

1

1st Thessalonians Introduction

Paul's Earliest Epistles

The first 100 years following Christ's birth can be accurately characterized as a century of transition. Its dawning concluded 400 years of silence from God and promptly introduced to the world the incarnate Word of God. Unfortunately, for God's people, the Jews had become far too accustomed to the four centuries of heavenly silence and consequently rejected the incarnate Word of God.

> *John 1:14 And the Word was made flesh, and dwelt among us, (and we beheld his glory, the glory as of the only begotten of the Father,) full of grace and truth.*

> *John 1:10 He was in the world, and the world was made by him, and the world knew him not. 11 He came unto his own, and his own received him not.*

This period also witnessed a monumental spiritual struggle. This struggle involved the transitioning from an extensive emphasis upon God's Law to prominence placed upon God's grace. One would think the Jews would have accepted and welcomed God's message of grace, but most agonized over the thought of relinquishing their traditions and trusting in the Lord Jesus Christ as Saviour. They failed to realize that the primary purpose of the Law was to serve as a schoolmaster preparing and pointing them to the Lord Jesus Christ as the justifier of all those who repent of their sin.

> *Galatians 3:23 But before faith came, we were kept under the law, shut up unto the faith which should afterwards be revealed. 24*

*Wherefore **the law was our schoolmaster to bring us unto Christ,** that we might be justified by faith. 25 But after that faith is come, we are no longer under a schoolmaster.*

The Jews not only rejected the incarnate Word but unashamedly scoffed at God's amazing grace. The Gentiles, however, joyfully received both *(Acts 28:23-29).*

*Acts 28:28 Be it known therefore unto you, that **the salvation of God is sent unto the Gentiles,** and that **they will hear it.***

God determined to use the Gentiles to provoke the nation of Israel to jealousy *(Romans 11:11).* As a result of God's redirected attention, the schism already existing between Jew and Gentile was further compounded due to the Gentiles' reception of Christ and the ensuing churches that blossomed and flourished. While some Jews readily welcomed the wall of partition being broken down between Jews and Gentiles in Christ *(Ephesians 2:14-18),* others aggressively attempted to thwart this transition through every means possible.

*Ephesians 2:14 For he is our peace, who hath **made both one, and hath broken down the middle wall of partition between us;** 15 Having abolished in his flesh the enmity, even the law of commandments contained in ordinances; for to make in himself of twain **one new man,** so making peace; 16 And that he might **reconcile both unto God in one body by the cross,** having slain the enmity thereby: 17 And came and preached peace to you which were afar off, and to them that were nigh. 18 **For through him we both have access by one Spirit** unto the Father.*

This newfound Church (uniting Jews and Gentiles into one body) introduced a stumblingblock as it relates to Bible prophecy. The Old Testament prophets accompanied by the Lord's earthly words directed **the Jewish nation** to prepare for dark days, days of trouble, just prior to the return of their Messiah and the establishment of His 1,000 year Kingdom. On the other hand, Paul's message to believers in the Church differed considerably by offering a certain and sure hope. Through the revelation given to the apostle Paul, he introduced "a mystery" that foretold the Church being taken out in its own unique departure prior to the time that God would redirect His attention to Israel.

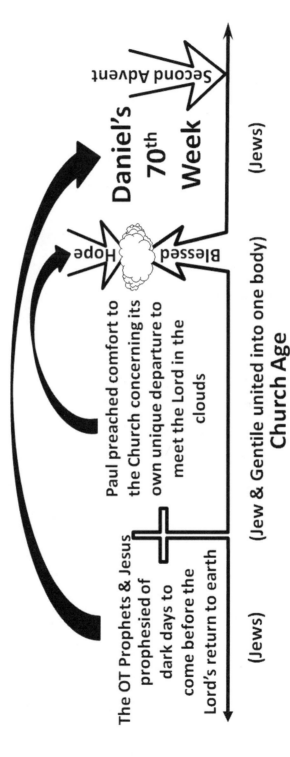

Distinct Messengers with Two Distinct Programs

The OT Prophets & Jesus prophesied of dark days to come before the Lord's return to earth

(Jews)

Paul preached comfort to the Church concerning its own unique departure to meet the Lord in the clouds

(Jew & Gentile united into one body) Church Age

Hope
Blessed

Daniel's 70th Week

Second Advent

(Jews)

[Chart 1.01]

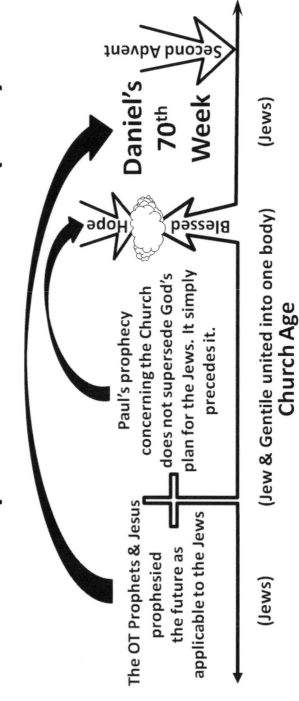

Paul's Prophecy Precedes
NOT Supersedes Previous Prophecy

Second Advent

Daniel's
70th
Week

(Jews)

[Chart 1.02]

Hope   Blessed

Paul's prophecy
concerning the Church
does not supersede God's
plan for the Jews. It simply
precedes it.

(Jew & Gentile united into one body)
Church Age

The OT Prophets & Jesus
prophesied
the future as
applicable to the Jews

(Jews)

© www.KJB1611.com

There is no debate concerning God's promise to the Church; the primary debate revolves around its timing (before, during, or after Daniel's Seventieth Week) and whether God intends to rekindle the distinctions between the nation of Israel and the Church. If the Lord reintroduces distinctions between Jew and Gentile within the Body of Christ on earth, He contradicts His word given to the Church through the apostle Paul *(Galatians 3:28, Colossians 3:11)*.

Corinth and Thessalonica

Every astute Bible student recognizes Paul's writings as the principal epistles directed toward the Church and the present Church Age. Within these writings, Christians find the primary epistles containing details of Christ's mysterious return for the Church. These epistles were written to the believers in the cities of Corinth and Thessalonica. It is important to note that both of these cities contained an influential Jewish population at the time of Paul's writings. For example, notice the unfolding of events in Thessalonica:

> [T]he prophetic plan *applicable to the Jews* had not been **superseded** but would be **preceded** by a prophetic plan unknown to past generations.

*Acts 17:1 Now when they had passed through Amphipolis and Apollonia, **they came to Thessalonica,** where was **a synagogue of the Jews**:*

This chapter describes the conduct of the *unbelieving* Jews of Thessalonica as they witnessed the success of the gospel preaching. These unbelieving Jews disapproved of the message and stooped to unfathomable lows in order to persecute, persuade, and deceive. The hostility became so pervasive that the church in Thessalonica shipped Paul and Silas to Berea in the dark of night.

*Acts 17:10 And **the brethren immediately sent away Paul and Silas by night unto Berea:** who coming thither went into the synagogue of the Jews.*

The hearts of the Bereans proved to be more fertile soil for the seed of God's word. Unlike the masses in Thessalonica, these people received the word with all readiness of mind. However, the Jews in Thessalonica sent forth some vocal unbelievers to stir up the Bereans, causing Paul to be yet again sent away.

> *Acts 17:13 But when **the Jews of Thessalonica** had knowledge that the word of God was preached of Paul at Berea, they **came thither also, and stirred up the people.** 14 And then **immediately the brethren sent away Paul** to go as it were to the sea: but Silas and Timotheus abode there still.*

The City of Corinth

Similar to Thessalonica, Corinth also consisted of a formidable Jewish population. The book of Acts points to one possible reason for this Jewish enclave: the Jews were forced to depart from Rome *(Acts 18:2)* and many may have found refuge in Corinth. A segment of these Jews, after hearing the truth, believed the gospel preaching. Others chose to make insurrection against Paul and brought him to the judgment seat claiming that he taught that the Jews should worship God contrary to the Law. If this proof was not sufficient evidence, Paul offered another identifier of the strong Jewish influence in Corinth when he wrote to them concerning *"our fathers."*

> *1 Corinthians 10:1 Moreover, brethren, I would not that ye should be ignorant, how that all **our fathers** were under the cloud, and all passed through the sea.*

Why would the Lord lead Paul to unveil the prophetic blueprint *for the Church* to the inhabitants of these two cities? As to the Corinthians, it was important for them to realize that the prophetic plan *applicable to the Jews* had not been **superseded** but would be **preceded** by a prophetic plan unknown to past generations. This teaching paralleled the teaching of the Jew/Gentile body to which it pertained, which also was virtually unknown until Paul's writings. Thessalonica, on the other hand, needed to hear these same truths for completely different reasons.

The City of Thessalonica

The Jews in Thessalonica ruthlessly reacted to the message of God's grace preached by Paul. On one account, we read of a letter written as though from Paul suggesting that the believers were missing the Day of Christ *(2 Thessalonians 2:2)*. The prime suspects for the forgery or forgeries written in his name pointed directly at the Jewish population who attempted to withstand Paul. In turn, the Lord led Paul to spring-board from these falsehoods to establish and distinguish the entirety of God's prophetic plan both for the Church (Gentiles and Jews who are in Christ) and the Jews of the future.

In these two Thessalonian letters, Paul referenced both the catching away of the Church (aka the Blessed Hope of *Titus 2:13*) and the Second Advent (Christ's return to establish His earthly Kingdom). In these epistles, Paul transitioned from one event to the other, at times with no forewarning. This is especially evident in First Thessalonians chapter 5 and Second Thessalonians chapters 1 and 2. All of the prophetic teachers today espousing the varied misinterpretations fail to understand or purposely ignore this context concerning the early church in Thessalonica.

The Coming for the Church Versus the Second Coming

In both First and Second Thessalonians, the Lord led Paul to thwart the influence of the unbelieving Jews by emphasizing Christ's coming *for the Church*. For example:

- *"...in the presence of our Lord Jesus Christ **at his coming?**" (1 Thessalonians 2:19)*
- *"...**at the coming** of our Lord Jesus Christ with all his saints." (1 Thessalonians 3:13)*
- *"...which are alive and remain **unto the coming of the Lord**..."* *(1 Thessalonians 4:15)*
- *"...preserved blameless **unto the coming of our Lord Jesus Christ**." (1 Thessalonians 5:23)*
- *"...**the coming of our Lord Jesus Christ**, and...our gathering together unto him," (2 Thessalonians 2:1)*

As is evident, the emphasis of Paul's epistles overwhelmingly focuses upon Christ's return for the Church; however, the two Thessalonian epistles also uniquely point toward the Second Advent. Here are three instances:

- *"...**the day of the Lord so cometh** as a thief in the night." (1 Thessalonians 5:2)*
- *"...**the Lord Jesus shall be revealed from heaven** with his mighty angels," (2 Thessalonians 1:7)*
- *"...whom the Lord...shall destroy **with the brightness of his coming**:" (2 Thessalonians 2:8)*

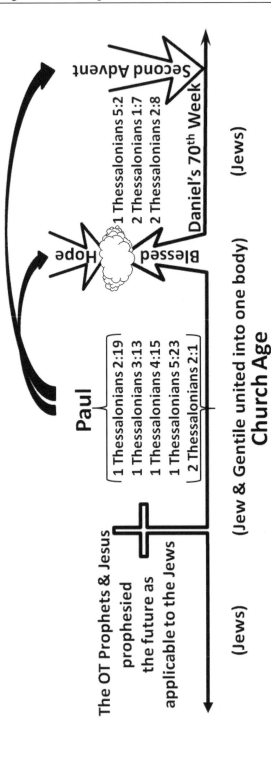

Paul's Prophecy: Dual Fulfillment by Two Distinct Groups

Unlike the Church's Blessed Hope, the Second Advent has been consistently prophesied as far back as the book of Genesis. This stark contrast cannot be overstated, nor can its significance underestimated! Christ's return for the Church involves delivering Christians by their simultaneous removal from the earth. On the other hand, **the Second Coming** of Christ to earth delivers the Jews from their enemies by finally destroying those who seek their extinction. The end results:

- **the Blessed Hope = the Church in Heaven, and**
- **the Second Advent = the Jews in an earthly Kingdom**

Christ's return in vengeance at the Second Advent is completely distinct from His return for the Church. Yet, both take center stage in the epistles Paul wrote to the Thessalonians. Paul only mentions the Rapture for the first four chapters of First Thessalonians and then the Second Advent interchangeably from chapter five into Second Thessalonians.

Why did a people who had no need that Paul write unto them concerning *"the times and the seasons" (1 Thessalonians 5:1)* have so much need that Paul write to them concerning the makeup of these two unique and independent prophetic plans? These epistles definitively answer this question for those sincerely seeking the truth. In order to grasp this truth, each chapter must be considered independently as well as collectively. Keep these charts in mind as you read this brief commentary on the prophetic significance of First and Second Thessalonians.

Paul's Thessalonian Writings Pointing to Christ's Coming for the Church	
1 Thessalonians 2:19	"…in the presence of our Lord Jesus Christ at his coming?"
1 Thessalonians 3:13	"…at the coming of our Lord Jesus Christ with all his saints."
1 Thessalonians 4:15	"…which are alive and remain unto the coming of the Lord…"
1 Thessalonians 5:23	"…preserved blameless unto the coming of our Lord Jesus Christ."
2 Thessalonians 2:1	"…the coming of our Lord Jesus Christ, and…our gathering together unto him,"
	[Chart 1.04a]

Paul's Thessalonian Writings Pointing to the Second Advent	
1 Thessalonians 5:2	"…the day of the Lord so cometh as a thief in the night."
2 Thessalonians 1:7	"…the Lord Jesus shall be revealed from heaven with his mighty angels,"
2 Thessalonians 2:8	"…whom the Lord…shall destroy with the brightness of his coming:"
	[Chart 1.04b]

2

Patiently Waiting

First Thessalonians Chapter 1

A s the apostolic days came to a close, three interrelated virtues remained paramount for the New Testament Church. They were *faith, hope,* and *charity (1 Corinthians 13:13)*. A studious reading of Paul's epistles finds praise given to the churches exhibiting these virtues. Paul testified as much concerning the Thessalonians when he praised their *"work of faith, and labour of love, and patience of hope."* As it pertains to the prophetic study at hand, one of these virtues stands out as being particularly significant—the Thessalonians' *"patience of hope."*

> *1 Thessalonians 1:3 Remembering without ceasing your work of faith, and labour of love, and **patience of hope** in our Lord Jesus Christ, in the sight of God and our Father;*

The apostle Paul praised the Thessalonian believers for their patience. Historically, the word *patience* is closely associated with the word *passion.* Passion, in turn, relates to suffering *(Acts 1:3)*. Thus, patience involves suffering or enduring times of difficulty. It is important to distinguish between *patience* and *longsuffering.* Patience speaks to the **quality** of one's endurance, whereas, longsuffering refers to the **quantity** (or length) of the endurance.

> The Thessalonian believers in the face of extreme adversity maintained their *hope*. But what was their hope? Paul's other teachings consistently associated it with a future resurrection.

The Thessalonian believers in the face of extreme adversity maintained their *hope*. But what was their hope? Paul's other teachings consistently associated it with a future resurrection *(Acts 23:6; Acts 24:15)*. For New Testament Church Age believers, this is what the Bible refers to as *"that blessed hope" (Titus 2:13)* that takes place when Christ returns for the Church *(1 Corinthians 15:51-58)*.

As these saints turned from their idols and trusted the finished work of Christ, they also set a watchful eye *"to wait for his* [God's] *Son from heaven."*

> *1 Thessalonians 1:9 For they themselves shew of us what manner of entering in we had unto you, and how ye **turned to God from idols to serve** the living and true God; 10 **And to wait for his Son from heaven**, whom he raised from the dead, even Jesus, which delivered us from the wrath to come.*

This waiting for the Lord's return patiently anticipated an event that the Bible indicates elsewhere could take place at any time. Not only did the Thessalonians adopt this view, but Paul commended them because they *"sounded out the word of the Lord"* in other places too.

> *1 Thessalonians 1:8 For **from you sounded out the word of the Lord** not only in Macedonia and Achaia, but also in every place your faith to God-ward is spread abroad; so that we need not to speak any thing.*

Paul hardly had to admonish those of Macedonia, Achaia, and beyond to be watchful for Jesus' return because of the faith spread from Thessalonica. The saints in Thessalonica anxiously anticipated Christ's return and were causing others to do the same.

Christians can easily understand why the Devil would want to destroy such faith. Those who anxiously await the Saviour's return are deeply affected by that certain hope. According to John's epistle, *"every man that hath this hope in him purifieth himself, even as he* [Jesus] *is pure."*

> Those who anxiously await the Saviour's return are deeply affected by that certain hope. According to John's epistle, *"every man that hath this hope in him purifieth himself, even as he* [Jesus] *is pure."*

*1 John 3:3 And **every man that hath this hope in him purifieth himself**, even as he is pure.*

Titus testified in a similar fashion as he directly and repeatedly associated looking for Jesus with godly living. Titus equated *"Looking for that blessed hope, and the glorious appearing of the great God and our Saviour Jesus Christ" (Titus 2:13)* with *"denying ungodliness and worldly lusts" (Titus 2:12)*, and living *"soberly, righteously, and godly" (Titus 2:12)*, along with being *"zealous of good works" (Titus 2:14)*.

> [F]aithful service and personal holiness *always* go hand in hand with an earnest expectation of the fulfillment of Bible prophecy and the expectant return of Christ.

*Titus 2:12 Teaching us that, **denying ungodliness and worldly lusts**, we should **live soberly, righteously, and godly, in this present world**; 13 **Looking for that blessed hope**, and the glorious appearing of the great God and our Saviour Jesus Christ; 14 Who gave himself for us, that he might redeem us from all iniquity, and purify unto himself a peculiar people, **zealous of good works**.*

In other words, faithful service and personal holiness *always* go hand in hand with an earnest expectation of the fulfillment of Bible prophecy and the expectant return of Christ. In fact, the underlying motivator for the unceasing *"work of faith, and labour of love"* was the Thessalonians' *"patience of hope."*

Chapter 1: Patience of Hope Waiting for God's Son	
1 Thessalonians 1:3	"patience of hope"
1 Thessalonians 1:10	"wait for his Son from heaven"
1 John 3:3	this hope causes a purifying of self
Titus 2:12-13	"Looking for that blessed hope" causes us to "live soberly, righteously, and godly"
Titus 2:13-14	"Looking for that blessed hope" causes us to become "a peculiar people, zealous of good works"
	[Chart 1.11]

If this hope could be destroyed or even significantly diminished, their steadfastness in labour would be weakened. The same holds true today! The Christian's faithful service and purity of heart corresponds directly to his watchfulness for and expectation of Christ's return.

It comes as no surprise that spawns of Satan attacked such faith in Thessalonica (see *2 Thessalonians 2:1-2*). Likewise, it should be evident why such faith has come under increasing attack today as we see the day approaching *(Hebrews 10:25)*! Some wonder how one can see the day approaching if Christ's return for the Church does not involve

> The visible indication of the times is seen only in the spiritual condition of men's hearts not in some outward celestial manifestations.

signs. Simply read Paul's *last days* description (i.e., *2 Timothy 3:1-13*) and you have your answer. The visible indication of the times is seen only in the spiritual condition of men's hearts not in some outward celestial manifestations.

*2 Timothy 3:1 This know also, that **in the last days perilous times shall come.***

*2 Timothy 3:13 But **evil men and seducers shall wax worse and worse**, deceiving, and being deceived.*

The description also shows itself as open-ended: men become *"worse and worse."* When are things bad enough? When God says they have become "worse-enough"!

3

Joys and Crowns Are Coming

First Thessalonians Chapter 2

Patience pays off! The *patience of hope* mentioned in chapter 1 that led the believers of Thessalonica to labour in the Lord would one day yield great dividends. Paul pointed to such an outcome as he again mentioned the Lord's return for His Church in this first epistle to the Thessalonians. The message: the Christian's faithfulness would be directly affected by his continued hope in the Saviour's return. This faithfulness will be rewarded when Christ comes to gather His saints.

> *1 Thessalonians 2:19 For **what is our hope, or joy, or crown of rejoicing**? Are not even ye in the presence of our Lord Jesus Christ at his coming?*

What was Paul's expected reward? What was his joy or crown of rejoicing? It was the people to whom he was writing. They were his reward; his *"glory and joy" (1 Thessalonians 2:20)*. They were his *"work in the Lord" (1 Corinthians 9:1)*. Paul's expectation of Christ's soon return caused him to faithfully preach the gospel. Those who trusted Christ through Paul's preaching would join Paul in Heaven. These believers are a part of Paul's reward for faithfulness. Praise the Lord that this truth expands beyond Paul to all

> Paul's expectation of Christ's soon return caused him to faithfully preach the gospel. Those who trusted Christ through Paul's preaching would join Paul in Heaven. These believers are a part of Paul's reward for faithfulness.

believers throughout the Church Age. The Christians' crown of rejoicing or joy includes seeing those whom we have affected with the truth join us in meeting Christ at His return.

2 Corinthians 1:14 *As also ye have acknowledged us in part, that **we are your rejoicing, even as ye also are ours in the day of the Lord Jesus.***

Philippians 4:1 *Therefore, my brethren dearly beloved and longed for, **my joy and crown**, so stand fast in the Lord, my dearly beloved.*

History provides an appropriate illustration of an unnamed young man who died shortly after coming to Christ. On his deathbed, this young man lamented of having no more time to witness to others. His testimony, shared in a sermon by A. G. Upham and heard by Charles Luther, later became the foundation for the following song in 1877.

Must I Go, and Empty-Handed?

Must I go, and empty-handed?—
Thus my dear Redeemer meet?
Not one day of service give Him,
Lay no trophy at His feet?

Not at death I shrink nor falter,
For my Saviour saves me now;
But to meet Him empty-handed! —
Thought of that now clouds my brow!

Oh, the years of sinning wasted,
Could I but recall them now,
I would give them to my Saviour:
To His will I'd gladly bow.

Oh, ye saints! arouse; be earnest!
Up and work while yet 'tis day,
Ere the night of death o'ertake you!
Strive for souls while yet you may.

Refrain
Must I go, and empty-handed?—
Must I meet my Saviour so!—
Not one soul with which to greet Him?
Must I empty-handed go?

4

Returning to the Father with ALL His Saints

First Thessalonians Chapter 3[1]

The New Testament Church lives together, serves together, loves together, rejoices together, reaps rewards together, and one day will leave together to meet Christ in the clouds. After we are gathered unto Christ in the clouds, we will follow Him into the presence of the Father. Carefully read this final verse in the chapter before we more fully consider its content and context.

> *1 Thessalonians 3:13 To the end he may stablish your hearts unblameable in holiness before God, even our Father, at the coming of our Lord Jesus Christ with all his saints.*

Chapter 3 of First Thessalonians ends with this commentary concerning the commencement of the Day of Christ as the Church Age concludes, but only after establishing a rather interesting foundation earlier in the chapter. The brotherly love binding one believer to another serves as the primary identifier of any true New Testament believer. Even prior to Christ's crucifixion, resurrection, and ascension, the Lord attested to such

> The New Testament Church lives together, serves together, loves together, rejoices together, reaps rewards together, and one day will leave together to meet Christ in the clouds.

[1] A special thanks to John Wright for his invaluable input with this chapter.

a bond when He said, *"By this shall all men know that ye are my disciples, if ye have love one to another" (John 13:35).* Following the commencement of the New Testament Church, the beloved apostle John re-

> From start to finish of First Thessalonians chapter 3, the mutual love binding brother to brother in the Lord permeates Paul's message.

peatedly emphasized this truth in his epistles *(1 John 2:10-11; 1 John 3:10-19; 1 John 4:20-21).*

From start to finish of First Thessalonians chapter 3, the mutual love binding brother to brother in the Lord permeates Paul's message. He began the chapter by reminding the saints that he sent Timotheus to establish them and comfort them concerning their faith.

> *1 Thessalonians 3:2 And **sent Timotheus**, our brother, and minister of God, and our fellowlabourer in the gospel of Christ, **to establish you, and to comfort you concerning your faith:***

These believers had experienced tremendous affliction and the apostle Paul desired that they would not be moved by their difficulties.

> *1 Thessalonians 3:3 That **no man should be moved by these afflictions**: for yourselves know that we are appointed thereunto.*

Paul reminded them that he had warned of such impending troubles but wanted to ensure that the tempter had not caused them to veer off course.

> *1 Thessalonians 3:4 For verily, when we were with you, **we told you before that we should suffer tribulation**; even as it came to pass, and ye know.*

Paul followed this by proving that everything concerning Christianity is intertwined. For this reason, Paul pointed out that the Thessalonian believers' failure to be stedfast in their faith could cause Paul's very labour to have been expended in vain.

> *1 Thessalonians 3:5 For this cause, when I could no longer forbear, I sent to know your faith, **lest by some means the tempter have tempted you, and our labour be in vain.***

As the epistle states, Timotheus returned to Paul with a glowing report concerning the Thessalonian believers *(1 Thessalonians 3:6).* This report became a great source of comfort *(1 Thessalonians 3:6-7)*, hope *(1 Thessalonians 3:8)*, thankfulness *(1 Thessalonians 3:9)*, and joy *(1 Thessalonians 3:9)*. This encouraging report kindled an even greater desire in both Paul and the believers of Thessalonica to see each other face-to-face *(1 Thessalonians 3:6, 10)*. It was the apostle's desire that God Himself and our Lord Jesus Christ would direct Paul again to visit these dear saints of Thessalonica *(1 Thessalonians 3:11-12)*. Paul concluded by reminding these faithful Christians that a day was approaching when all of Christ's saints would have a glorious reunion in the clouds. This gathering would be followed by a supernatural transport into Heaven to stand *"before God, even our Father."*

> *1 Thessalonians 3:13 To the end he may stablish your hearts unblameable in holiness **before God, even our Father, at the coming of our Lord Jesus Christ with all his saints.***

At first glance, Bible students might feel tempted to force this final passage of chapter 3 into a Second Advent return application. After all, it is true that the armies of Heaven will return to earth WITH Christ at His Second Advent *(Revelation 19:14)*. Additionally, both Enoch *(Jude 14-15)* and Zechariah *(Zechariah 14:5)* prophesied of the saints' joint venture to return WITH Christ at that time. Context, however, suggests a completely different meaning and application for the passage in First Thessalonians chapter 3.

This passage refers to a coming but this coming *(John 14:6 "cometh unto the Father")* refers to Christ's return to the Father *"with all his saints"* after the saint's have been gathered to Christ in the clouds. This same truth (that Christ will return to the Father with all His saints) is the focus of Paul's teachings expressed to the believers in Colosse, but from an even more unique perspective. Not only will the dead in Christ return with Jesus when He returns to the Father with the Church, but we too (those alive at His coming) will *"appear with him* [Christ] *in glory"* at Christ's coming and appearing before the Father.

> Paul concluded by reminding these faithful Christians that a day was approaching when all of Christ's saints would have a glorious reunion in the clouds.

*Colossians 3:4 When Christ, who is our life, **shall appear**, then shall ye also appear with him in glory.*

When Christ returns to the Father, we also shall appear WITH HIM IN GLORY. *Glory* does not refer to the Christian's state of being (glorified bodies) but to the Father's location (Heaven). First Timothy plainly points out the location of *"glory"* as Christ's abode after He ascended back to the Father *(Ephesians 4:10).*

*1 Timothy 3:16 And without controversy great is the mystery of godliness: **God was** manifest in the flesh, justified in the Spirit, seen of angels, preached unto the Gentiles, believed on in the world, **received up into glory**.*

Up until this point in First Thessalonians, much of the apostle Paul's aim in teaching these believers of Thessalonica about the Lord's soon return was practical, devotional, or motivational in nature. Chapter 4 shifts the focus of First Thessalonians as the apostle begins the chapter with the word *"Furthermore."* In other words, chapter 4 offers a more in-depth discussion of a topic broached in the first three chapters.

> When Christ returns to the Father, we also shall appear WITH HIM IN GLORY. *Glory* does not refer to the Christian's state of being (glorified bodies) but to the Father's location (Heaven).

*1 Thessalonians 4:1 **Furthermore** then we beseech you, brethren, and exhort you by the Lord Jesus...*

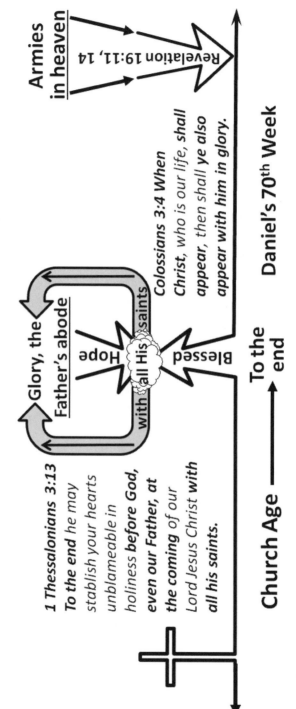

Christ Appears
WITH All His Saints

Armies in heaven

Revelation 19:11, 14

[Chart 1.31]

Colossians 3:4 When Christ, who is our life, shall appear, then shall ye also appear with him in glory.

Daniel's 70th Week

Glory, the Father's abode

Hope

with all His saints

Blessed

1 Thessalonians 3:13 To the end he may stablish your hearts unblameable in holiness before God, even our Father, at the coming of our Lord Jesus Christ with all his saints.

To the end

Church Age

© www.KJB1611.com

Paul expounds upon the Pre-tribulation Rapture in all eight chapters of First & Second Thessalonians

5

Be Not Ignorant!

First Thessalonians Chapter 4

Paul's epistles typically begin with doctrinal truths followed by a practical application of those truths. Paul's first epistle to the believers at Thessalonica, however, deviates from his normal tendencies. This deviation pertains especially to God's prophetic plan for the Church. In fact, Paul's teaching becomes more in-depth and doctrinally applicable as the reader progresses from one chapter to the next.

Similar to Paul's other epistles, First Thessalonians chapter 4 begins with encouraging words for God's saints. In this segment, Paul admonishes believers to abstain from sorrowing for departed loved ones in the same fashion as the world sorrows for their deceased loved ones. These believers in Thessalonica were most likely troubled after watching family and friends die from the persecutions and afflictions *(1 Thessalonians 1:6; 1 Thessalonians 2:14-16; 1 Thessalonians 3:2-5)*. These admonitions to valiantly endure tribulations also apply to those who will be persecuted and afflicted PRIOR to the Rapture and the commencement of Daniel's Seventieth Week.

> These admonitions to valiantly endure tribulations also apply to those who will be persecuted and afflicted PRIOR to the Rapture and the commencement of Daniel's Seventieth Week.

It is important for believers not to view death in similar fashion to the world's view so Paul sets the record straight. Ignorance concerning the future of these departed saints could have proven extremely detrimental to Paul's ministry during the Church's embryonic period.

Paul began with a practical point of encouragement but soon yielded to a doctrinal dissertation concerning the future of the New Testament Church. Though the subject matter may appear to shift abruptly from **1 Thessalonians 4:12** to **1 Thessalonians 4:13**, prophecy was a subject commonly discussed by Paul with these believers (both in written correspondence and in personal conversations). In Paul's second letter, he felt compelled to remind these believers of these personal discussions:

2 Thessalonians 2:5 *Remember ye not, that, **when I was yet with you, I told you these things**?*

As it pertains to God's unique prophetic plan for the Church, two truths stand out in the final six verses of chapter 4: (1) believers, whether alive or asleep in Jesus, will rise to meet the Lord at His return for them, and (2) Jesus Himself will return for the Church but will descend no further than the clouds in the sky. Some Bible students wish that Paul had gone a little further with his prophecy to definitively identify where Christians head after the Rapture (up to Heaven or back to earth). In the context, Paul assures the believer of this one thing: where the Lord goes, we go: *"so shall we ever be with the Lord."*

The Pre-tribulation believer teaches that we meet the Lord in the air and return with Him into Heaven. On earth at that time, the Lord redirects His attention toward the nation of Israel as

> [T]he Post-tribulationist would state that the Lord's coming for the Church is a vertical coming followed by a horizontal coming to establish His Kingdom upon the earth.

Daniel's Seventieth Week commences. Most Post-tribulationist teachers claim that the Church meets the Lord in the clouds only to return to earth. From the Lord's perspective, the Post-tribulationist would state that the Lord's coming for the Church is a vertical coming followed by a horizontal coming to establish His Kingdom upon the earth. Unfortunately for them, the Post-tribulation position contradicts the plain teaching of scripture in Revelation chapter 19 in two crucial matters. First, at Christ's Second Coming, Revelation points out that Heaven opens and the Lord descends; and secondly, *"the armies **which were in heaven"*** follow the Lord on white horses.

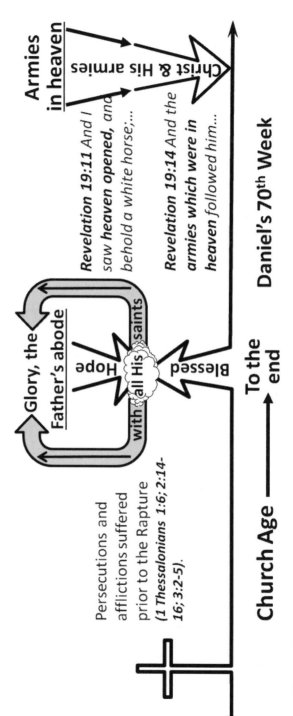

Christ Returns to Earth WITH All His Armies

Armies in heaven

Christ & His armies

Revelation 19:11 And I saw heaven opened, and behold a white horse;...

Revelation 19:14 And the armies which were in heaven followed him...

Daniel's 70th Week

Glory, the Father's abode

Hope

Blessed

with all His saints

To the end

Persecutions and afflictions suffered prior to the Rapture (1 Thessalonians 1:6; 2:14-16; 3:2-5).

Church Age

[Chart 1.41]

© www.KJB1611.com

Revelation 19:11 And I saw heaven opened, and behold a white horse; and he that sat upon him was called Faithful and True, and in righteousness he doth judge and make war.

*Revelation 19:14 And **the armies which were in heaven followed him** upon white horses, clothed in fine linen, white and clean.*

Thus, both the Lord and His armies leave Heaven directly to earth, with no indication of any time allotted for gathering His army in the clouds first. The only way for any type of Post-tribulation scenario to work is for the Rapture to take place between the two verses mentioned above (which none of the Post-tribulation teachers **yet** claim).

The Bibles says that Jesus leaves Heaven (verse 11) for the battle to ensue upon the earth. The armies, which are **in Heaven,** follow Him **from Heaven** (verse 14), not after meeting Him in the clouds at some supposed Post-tribulation Rapture. The Bible offers the Bible student the necessary specifics for good reason—the truth always brings to light the errors taught by those with agendas or misconceptions. Heaven opens and the Lord descends with the armies following him *"which were in heaven,"* not in the clouds and certainly not on earth. There is no disputing the facts!

> [T]he Church's Blessed Hope, involves two major parts: (1) the resurrection and subsequent change of those dead in Christ, and (2) the changing of those alive at the time of Christ's return.

We Shall All Be Changed

Many of the most vocal opponents of the Pre-tribulation Rapture mistakenly claim that *1 Thessalonians 4:13-18* serves as the only "proof" text for teaching a Pre-tribulation Rapture. Even if this were the case, such a clear and precise passage on a particular doctrine would surely make it worthy of acceptance. However, the Lord provided several other witnesses to the truth of this mystery. One such witness is found in **1 Corinthians 15:51-58** where the Lord offers a more in-depth account of the bodily redemption that takes place at Christ's return for Church Age believers.

> *1 Corinthians 15:51 Behold, I shew you a mystery; **We shall not all sleep, but we shall all be changed**, 52 In a moment, in the twinkling*

*of an eye, at the last trump: for the trumpet shall sound, and **the dead shall be raised incorruptible**, and **we shall be changed**.*

According to this passage, the Rapture, also known as the Church's Blessed Hope, involves two major parts: (1) the resurrection and subsequent change of those dead in Christ, and (2) the changing of those alive at the time of Christ's return.

These truths, albeit to a lesser extent, are similarly conveyed in *1 Thessalonians 4:13-14*. In both passages, the dead in Christ are said to be *asleep*.[1]

The souls of those who are dead in Christ are already in the presence of the Lord Jesus Christ *(2 Corinthians 5:8)*. They currently await their return to obtain

> [T]he Church's Blessed Hope, involves two major parts: (1) the resurrection and subsequent change of those dead in Christ, and (2) the changing of those alive at the time of Christ's return.

glorified bodies when they come in the clouds with Christ at His coming for the Church. The bodies of Christians who have died have been laid to rest awaiting their resurrection and change.

> *1 Thessalonians 4:13 But I would not have you to be **ignorant**, brethren, concerning them which are asleep, that ye sorrow not, even as others which have **no hope**. 14 For if we believe that Jesus died and rose again, **even so them also which sleep in Jesus will God bring with him**.*

The change of those alive at the time of Christ's return *"shall not prevent them which are asleep."* Though some have been critical of the wording of this passage, the honest and faithful Bible student can clearly glean that the word *prevent* means to go *before*.[2]

> *1 Thessalonians 4:15 For this we say unto you by the word of the Lord, that **we which are alive and remain** unto the coming of the Lord shall not prevent them which are asleep.*

---

[1] This truth does not teach or imply the false doctrine of "soul sleep," for these passages refer to the *bodies* as asleep and not the souls or spirits of departed loved ones.

[2] See **Psalm 88:13** *But unto thee have I cried, O LORD; and in the morning shall my prayer prevent thee.*

After the bodies of the dead are resurrected, those who remain alive until Christ's coming are promised to be changed in the twinkling of an eye *(1 Corinthians 15:52)*. This change is identified elsewhere as the *adoption* which takes place when the Lord redeems the mortal body and adopts and glorifies it.

> **Romans 8:23** *And not only they, but ourselves also, which have the firstfruits of the Spirit, even we ourselves groan within ourselves,* ***waiting for the adoption, to wit, the redemption of our body.***

Those who have trusted Jesus Christ as Saviour are presently "two-thirds redeemed." On the surface, that concept may seem awkward, but when all things are considered in the light of scripture, the confusion disappears. Man is a three-part being, made up of spirit, soul, and body *(1 Thessalonians 5:23)*. Our *souls* have been redeemed by the blood of the Lamb. Our *spirits* have been quickened or made alive by the Holy Ghost. Our bodies, on the other hand, are *"vile" (Philippians 3:21)*, *"corruptible" (1 Corinthians 15:53)*, *"mortal" (1 Corinthians 15:54)*, and remain in need of redemption. The adoption is the redemption and glorification of the body.

When Christ returns, He will give us the change for which we have been waiting. Our bodies will be redeemed *(Romans 8:23)* and we will be changed *(1 Corinthians 15:51-52)*. We will truly be like Christ *(1 John 3:2)* because our vile bodies will be changed to *"be fashioned like unto his glorious body" (Philippians 3:21)*. This change is unique to the adoption which takes place at the Rapture of the Church. These changes are not typically the source of debate. Their timing, however, is. Unfortunately, far too many Bible teachers assume there is no way to precisely assess at what point in the prophetic time line this change will occur.

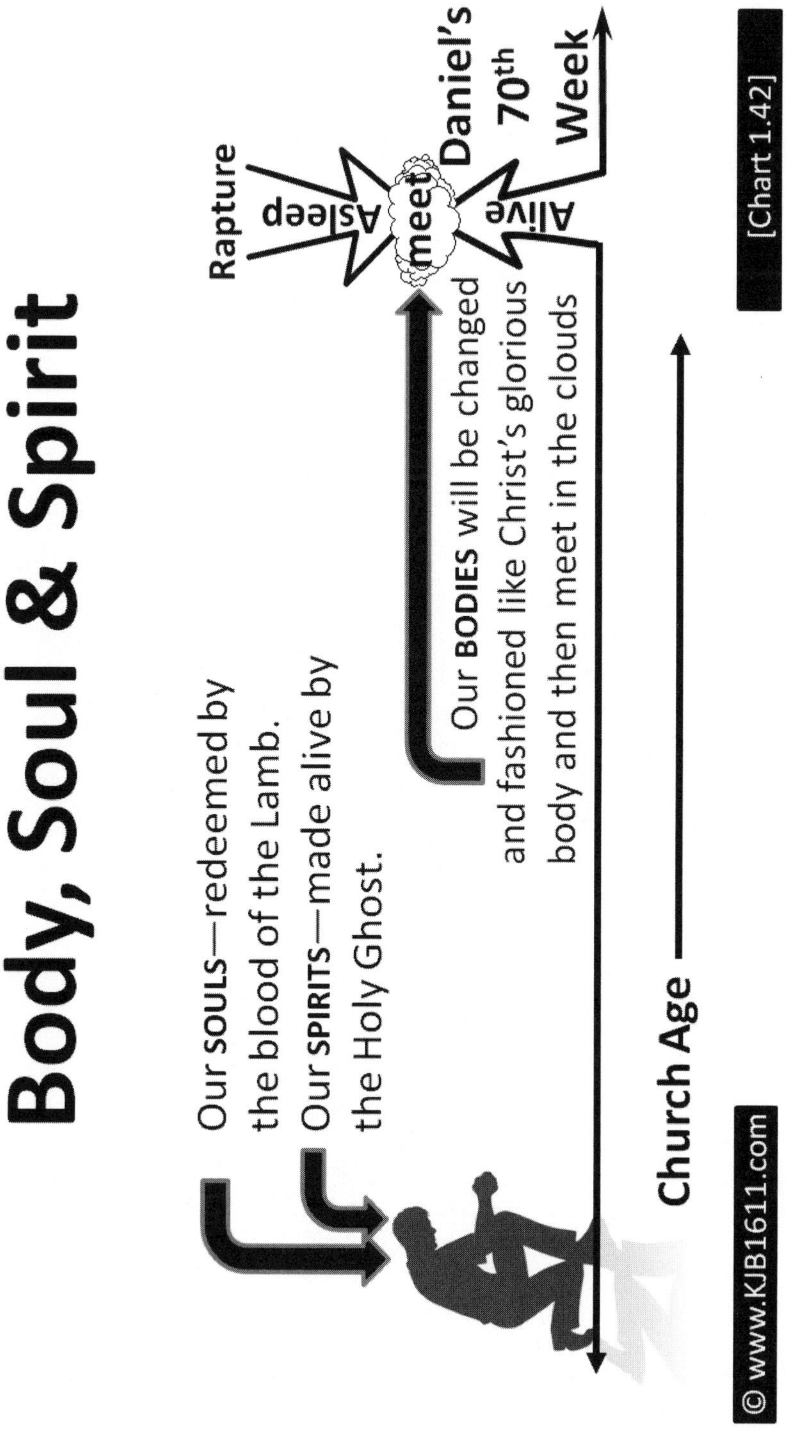
Body, Soul & Spirit
Our SOULS—redeemed by the blood of the Lamb.
Our SPIRITS—made alive by the Holy Ghost.
Our BODIES will be changed and fashioned like Christ's glorious body and then meet in the clouds
Rapture
Asleep
meet
Alive
Daniel's 70th Week
Church Age
© www.KJB1611.com
[Chart 1.42]

Where's the Church?

The Bible gives us all the information we need to understand the timing of future events. Daniel's Seventieth Week[3] offers a precise, definitive, and irrefutable demarcation. The book of Daniel specifically states that this *week of years* applies to *"thy* (Daniel's) *people" (Daniel 9:24)* which is Israel. Not one passage of scripture states nor even implies that this period was ever intended for the Church whose formation remained a mystery until the revelations given through Paul's epistles *(Ephesians 3:9-10)*.

Concerning this future *week of years*, several passages specifically mention Israel while the Church remains conspicuously absent. The Post-tribulationalist must force the Church into passages where the Church is NEVER mentioned. On the other hand, a Pre-tribulation Rapture accounts for the Church's absence. For one example among many, John repeatedly emphasized that Satan, when he is cast from Heaven at the midpoint of the Tribulation, persecutes the *woman (Revelation 12:6, 13, 17)*. This is the same "woman" whom God specifically protects *(Revelation 12:15, 16)*. The woman is identified as none other than the nation of Israel *(Revelation 12:1-4)*. Why no mention of the Church in these and other pertinent passages?[4] Could it be because the Church is absent?

In addition to the Church's conspicuous absence, the future seven-year period revives distinctions between Israel and the Church eliminated within the present Body of Christ *(Galatians 3:28, Colossians 3:11)*. There are many other peculiar distinctions too. Those within the nations who survive the Tribulation and enter into the Kingdom will require the nourishment and benefit of the tree(s) of life for meat and

[3] See **Appendix #1** (*"Pinpointing Daniel's Seventy Weeks"*), and **Appendix #2** (*"Charting Daniel's Seventieth Week"*)
[4] Another example: Revelation chapters 6 through 18 cover Daniel's Seventieth Week with no mention of the Church on earth after Revelation chapter 3.

Where's the Church?

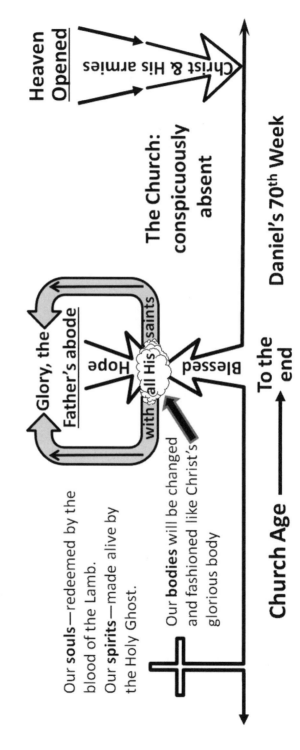

Our **souls**—redeemed by the blood of the Lamb.
Our **spirits**—made alive by the Holy Ghost.

Our **bodies** will be changed and fashioned like Christ's glorious body

Hope

Glory, the Father's abode

Blessed

with all His saints

Heaven Opened

Christ & His armies

The Church: conspicuously absent

Daniel's 70th Week

Church Age

To the end

[Chart 1.43]

healing *(Ezekiel 47:12; Revelation 22:2)*. This cannot apply to Christians with glorified bodies.

The Lord Himself Shall Descend

Yet another distinguishing feature of the Church's departure is that the Lord HIMSELF (without mention of the angels) will descend FROM HEAVEN for all Christians. Remember that every word of God is pure. The Bible does not simply say the Lord shall descend but purposefully and emphatically states the fact that the Lord **HIMSELF** will descend for His Church, indicating that, at this event, no one is sent on Christ's behalf to perform any task.

> *1 Thessalonians 4:16 For the Lord **himself** shall descend from heaven with a shout, with the voice of the archangel, and with the trump of God: and the dead in Christ shall rise first:*

There is no mention in Thessalonians (unlike Matthew chapter 24) of Christ **sending** angels to gather or remove God's people. Instead, the scripture plainly emphasizes that it will be Christ HIMSELF doing the gathering. Contrast this statement in Thessalonians with the passage in Matthew that prophesies that the Lord accompanies His angels who are **sent** for the purpose of gathering His elect (Israel) just prior to the Second Advent and the Day of the Lord.

> *Matthew 24:31 And **he shall send his angels** with a great sound of a trumpet, and they shall gather together his elect from the four winds, from one end of heaven to the other.*

As the evidence mounts, most of the arguments against these distinctions are exposed for ignoring or belittling God's precision and distinctions within His word. This is both unwise and dangerous. It is imperative to understand that the details of the Rapture remained a *mystery (1 Corinthians 15:51)* to mankind until the Lord revealed them to the apostle Paul. The doctrine of the Rapture does not show up before Paul's writings except in pictures, types, and insinuations.

Matthew, at the time of his writing, neither knew of nor wrote

> Matthew, at the time of his writing, neither knew of nor wrote of the New Testament Church's removal from the earth.

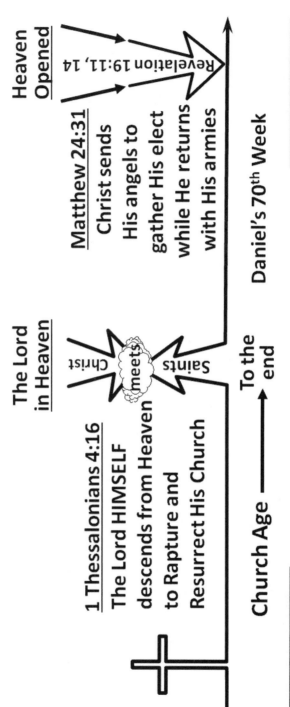

[Chart 1.44]

of the New Testament Church's removal from the earth. Paul clearly distinguishes between the Church's departure and the Second Advent gathering by pointing out that the Lord HIMSELF will come and get His Church. If this gathering at the Rapture is the same as Matthew chapter 24, why no mention by Paul of the armies following the Lord *(Revelation 19:14)*?

There is no general **catching up** in the days approaching the Second Advent. It is simply not a rapture. This is why the Lord sends His angels to *gather together* His elect for supernatural protection upon the earth. This protection takes place toward the end of Daniel's Seventieth Week and almost simultaneously with His return in vengeance on the Day of the Lord.

> There is no general **catching up** in the days approaching the Second Advent. It is simply not a rapture.

The context of Matthew's writing in the middle of chapter 24 delineates details of the conclusion of Daniel's Seventieth Week, the introduction of the Day of the Lord, and the Lord's Second Advent.

> *Matthew 24:29 Immediately after the tribulation of those days shall the* **sun** *be* **darkened,** *and the* **moon** *shall* **not give her light,** *and the* **stars** *shall* **fall** *from heaven, and the* **powers of the heavens** *shall be* **shaken:** *30* **And then** *shall appear the sign of the Son of man in heaven: and then shall all the tribes of the earth mourn, and they shall see the Son of man coming in the clouds of heaven with power and great glory.*

Matthew mentions the darkening of the sun just prior to the Lord's return correlating to the events mentioned in Joel and Acts. The Bible specifically says, "*The* **sun shall be turned into darkness,** *and the moon into blood,* **before the great and the terrible day of the LORD come** *(Joel 2:31).* Joel associates the darkening of the sun to the Day of the Lord. At the onset of the Day of the Lord, the Lord Jesus sends His angels to gather His elect. The Bible clearly defines His elect as Israel *(Isaiah 45:4)* and they must be gathered in haste as the Lord leads His armies to battle. Historically, the Lord *scattered* the nations (including Israel) to the winds through their captivities or general scatterings as an act of chastening resulting from their rejection of Him. [5]

---

[5] Here are four passages which reflect the *scattering* to the utmost corners of the

The Lord will gather His elect (Israel) from all the earth—*from the four winds, from one end of heaven to the other.* This passage is in no way synonymous with the Rapture of First Thessalonians chapter 4. In fact, there is no Rapture or catching away FROM the earth in *Matthew 24:31.* The heaven mentioned is the first heaven and not

> [T]here is no Rapture or catching away FROM the earth in *Matthew 24:31.*

the abode of God or His raptured saints. Contextually, there is also no gathering from the third Heaven of God's abode. [6]

> *Matthew 24:31 And **he shall send his angels** with a great sound of a trumpet, and they shall **gather together his elect from the four winds, from one end of heaven to the other.***

At Christ's Second Advent, He will send His angels to gather the elect from *the four winds of* (the first) *heaven.* The heaven mentioned in Matthew chapter 24 with the four winds is not the third Heaven of God's abode *(2 Corinthians 12:2)*, but the first heaven *(Jeremiah 49:36; Daniel 7:2, Daniel 8:8).*

---

earth using the four winds from the four quarters of heaven. They are said to be scattered into all the winds:

*Jeremiah 49:32 And their camels shall be a booty, and the multitude of their cattle a spoil: and **I will scatter into all winds them that are in the utmost corners**; and I will bring their calamity from all sides thereof, saith the LORD.*

*Jeremiah 49:36 And upon Elam will I bring **the four winds from the four quarters of heaven, and will scatter them toward all those winds**; and there shall be no nation whither the outcasts of Elam shall not come.*

*Ezekiel 5:10b ...the whole remnant of thee will I **scatter into all the winds.***

*Ezekiel 17:21 And all his fugitives with all his bands shall fall by the sword, and they that remain shall be **scattered toward all winds**: and ye shall know that I the LORD have spoken it.*

[6] Some Post-tribulationists assume that the mention of *heaven* means the third Heaven (God's abode); however, the context remains constant since the passage refers to the first heaven where the *winds* blow *(1 Kings 18:45, Psalm 78:26, Daniel 7:2, 8:8, 11:4). Jeremiah 49:36* clearly associates the four winds with the first heaven, *"I bring **the four winds from the four quarters of heaven"** and Zechariah 2:6* specifically refers to *"the four winds of the heaven."* The winds and the heavens refer to the first and not the *"third Heaven" (2 Corinthians 12:2).*

The distinct details make it obvious that **Matthew 24:31** is NOT the Rapture of the Church. This is especially obvious when one considers that the days identified in Matthew chapter 24 are likened to the days of Noah.[7] Those *taken away* (judged) in Noah's day are certainly the wicked; those protected—God's people.

> **Matthew 24:37 But as the days of Noe were, so shall also the coming of the Son of man be.** 38 *For as in the days that were before the flood they were eating and drinking, marrying and giving in marriage, until the day that Noe entered into the ark,* 39 *And* **knew not** *until the flood came, and* **took them all away; so shall also the coming of the Son of man be.** 40 *Then shall two be in the field; the* **one shall be taken,** *and the other left.* 41 *Two women shall be grinding at the mill; the* **one shall be taken,** *and the other left.*

Noah knew the flood was coming because God told him directly **(Genesis 7:4)**. Thus, those in verse 39 who were taken away and *"knew not"* cannot be referring to Noah and his family. In Noah's day, it was the unbelievers who were taken away or removed from the earth and *"so shall also the coming of the Son of man be"* **(Matthew 24:39)**. Noah and his family were gathered together for protection in the ark when the floods came. In like manner, God will gather His elect for protection when the floods of wrath issue forth upon an unbelieving world.

The heaven mentioned in Matthew chapter 24 with the four winds is not the third Heaven of God's abode **(2 Corinthians 12:2)**, but the first heaven **(Jeremiah 49:36; Daniel 7:2, Daniel 8:8)**.

Luke's gospel likewise points to Lot's protection from the wrath poured forth upon Sodom as a synopsis of the events surrounding the Lord's Second Advent. The angels will gather together the elect and protect them just as the angels gathered Lot and protected him from the destruction inflicted upon Sodom. The day the ANGELS gathered Lot, the destruction came.

---

[7] Unfortunately, many Pre-tribulation teachers have likened the protection of Noah and Lot as examples of the Rapture and God's supernatural protection toward the Church. Instead, these pictures, types, and details apply to the nation of Israel and their supernatural deliverance, NOT THE CHURCH.

*Luke 17:28 Likewise also **as it was in the days of Lot**; they did eat, they drank, they bought, they sold, they planted, they builded; 29 But **the same day that Lot went out of Sodom** it rained fire and brimstone from heaven, and **destroyed them all.** 30 Even thus shall it be in the day when the Son of man is revealed. 31 In that day, he which shall be upon the housetop, and his stuff in the house, let him not come down to take it away: and he that is in the field, let him likewise not return back. 32 Remember Lot's wife.*

The application of the truth to the Jews alive at Christ's Second Advent is that they should *"Remember Lot's wife" (Luke 17:32)*. In other words, they should be aware of the inherent dangers of looking back even to their beloved city as the angels seek to gather them for protection from the wrath to come. Lot and Noah are NOT pictures for the Church, but of those alive at the inception of the Day of the Lord. Unfortunately, these truths and pictures are consistently misapplied by teachers on both sides of the Pre-tribulation Rapture debate.

> Lot and Noah are NOT pictures for the Church, but of those alive at the inception of the Day of the Lord. Unfortunately, these truths and pictures are consistently misapplied by teachers on both sides of the Pre-tribulation Rapture debate.

The Meeting in the Air

No true Bible believer ever dismisses even the most seemingly insignificant details found in scripture. Though some points may seem inconsequential, a thorough study always reveals that God's word has purpose and plan for every word and punctuation mark, including the order in which they occur. Those who point to the original languages as the only trustworthy source seem to assume that God's preservation must have failed with the disintegration of the originals. God promises man that HIS WORDS will not pass away.[8] For instance, the Bible emphasizes the fact that at Christ's coming for the Church, Christians are caught up to meet Him *in the air.*

> *1 Thessalonians 4:17 Then we which are alive and remain shall be **caught up** together with them in the clouds, **to meet the Lord in the air**: and so shall we ever be with the Lord.*

---

[8] *Matthew 24:35 Heaven and earth shall pass away, but my words shall not pass away.*

There is no disputing the fact that the Rapture involves Church Age saints being caught up *in the clouds.* This is where the saved (whether dead in Christ or alive and remaining until Christ's return) meet together with their Saviour. At this return, the Lord Jesus does not actually set foot upon the earth—a detail distinguishing the Rapture from the Second Advent. Another distinguishing factor involves the question of destination for raptured saints. Where do they go—back to Heaven with Him (Pre-tribulation teaching) or only back to earth (Post-tribulation teaching)?

> At this return, the Lord Jesus does not actually set foot upon the earth—a detail distinguishing the Rapture from the Second Advent.

We have already seen how the Post-tribulation teaching contradicts the fact that the Lord's armies will leave Heaven when Christ leaves Heaven at the Second Advent *(Revelation 19:11, 14).*

The Second Advent presents a different sequence and scenario from the Rapture of Church Age saints. Christ does not stop at the clouds but returns all the way to earth with His armies in tow. In fact, the precise location of Christ's return at the Second Advent is clearly defined in passages like Acts chapter 1 and Zechariah chapter 14 as the Mount of Olives.

> *Acts 1:11 Which also said, Ye men of Galilee, why stand ye gazing up into heaven?* **this same Jesus, which is taken up from you into heaven, shall so come in like manner as ye have seen him go into heaven.** *12 Then returned they unto Jerusalem from* **the mount called Olivet,** *which is from Jerusalem a sabbath day's journey.*

> *Zechariah 14:4 And his feet shall stand in that day upon the* **mount of Olives,** *which is before Jerusalem on the east, and the mount of Olives shall cleave in the midst thereof toward the east and toward the west, and there shall be a very great valley; and half of the mountain shall remove toward the north, and half of it toward the south.*

The Bible makes clear distinctions between Christ's return to call out His Church and His Second Coming to the earth with His armies FROM HEAVEN. The Rapture involves the Lord taking the Church to His Heavenly abode, while the Second Advent serves as the introduction of Christ's earthly Kingdom.

So Shall We Ever Be with the Lord

Seemingly *new* doctrines frequently involve the repackaging and re-peating of doctrines previously taught and rejected by past genera-tions. Solomon stated as much when he concluded that *"there is no new thing under the sun" (Ecclesiastes 1:9)*. Unfortunately, the most egregious teachings become the most entrenched with the idea that their longevity somehow gives them a form of legitimacy.

There are innumerable instances where a false doctrine taught in the past is picked up and regurgitated by the current generation. The false doctrine known as *Kingdom Exclusion* is one such doctrine. This teaching was refuted by Sir Robert Anderson as early as 1914 and involves the idea that unfaithful Christians will receive their just chastening by missing out on the Lord's earthly millennial Kingdom.

> The Rapture involves the Lord taking the Church to His Heavenly abode, while the Second Advent serves as the introduction of Christ's earthly Kingdom.

To be perfectly clear, some teach that these believers missing the King-dom will instead suffer in the Lake of Fire for 1,000 years.

The answer to this heresy is so simple that it makes one wonder how anyone could espouse such a doctrine. According to *1 Thessalonians 4:17*, believers removed from the earth at the Rapture of the Church are said to *"ever be with the Lord."* Since every Christian will be with the Lord, how can a Christian be excluded from the millennial Kingdom or suffer in the Lake of Fire? Will the Lord Himself miss the millennial Kingdom to suffer with unfaithful Christians? And, if Jesus misses the Kingdom, would that not require all Christians to miss the Kingdom in order for all Christians to *"ever be with the Lord" (1 Thessalonians 4:17)*? In part, the false teaching of Kingdom Exclusion is based on a faulty un-derstanding of a passage in Second Timothy. Context determines mean-ing and false doctrines come from ignoring context.

> *2 Timothy 2:12 If we **suffer**, we shall also reign with him: if we **deny** him, he also will deny us:*

Some have wrongfully assumed that believers denied the opportu-ni-ty to *"reign"* with Christ must altogether miss the Kingdom. This simply is not the teaching here or elsewhere. The passage instead explains the means by which believers can *"reign"* or exercise *"authority"* over cities *(Luke 19:17)* in the millennial Kingdom. The error in interpretation comes from two assumptions: (1) the word *suffer* means the endurance of trials and persecutions and (2) the word *deny* means to pretend not to know someone or something.

> Since every Christian will be with the Lord, how can a Christian be excluded from the millennial Kingdom or suffer in the lake of fire? Will the Lord Himself miss the millennial Kingdom to suffer with unfaithful Christians?

The Lord teaches by both comparison and contrast, but it is quite obvious that the Lord's chosen method in this passage was *contrast*. The intended interpretation can only be found when the Bible student first acknowledges the *contrasts* found within the context. The chart following the subject passage delineates the original subject and the contrasting subject in each verse.

*2 Timothy 2:9 Wherein **I suffer trouble**, as an evil doer, **even unto bonds**; but the word of God is not bound. 10 Therefore **I endure all things** for the elect's sakes, **that they may also obtain the salvation** which is in Christ Jesus with eternal glory. 11 It is a faithful saying: For **if we be dead** with him, **we shall also live** with him: 12 **If we suffer**, we shall also reign with him: **if we deny him**, he also will deny us: 13 **If we believe not**, yet **he abideth faithful**: he cannot deny himself.*

Passage	Original Subject	Contrasting Subject
2 Timothy 2:9	Paul: "I suffer trouble... even unto bonds;"	Scripture: "but the word of God is not bound."
2 Timothy 2:10	Paul: "I endure all things"	The elect: "that they may... obtain the salvation"
2 Timothy 2:11	The Christian's present: "if we be dead"	The Christian's future: "we shall also live"
2 Timothy 2:12	The Christian's obedience: "If we suffer (him)"	The Christian's disobedience: "if we deny him,"

Passage	Original Subject	Contrasting Subject
2 Timothy 2:12	The Christian's reward: "we shall... reign"	The Christian's consequences: "he...will deny us:" (Context: a reign)
2 Timothy 2:13	The UNfaithful Christian: "If we believe not,"	The faithful Saviour: "he abideth faithful:"
		[Chart 1.45]

According to the context, the plain truth is that every Christian chooses to *suffer* or *deny* the Saviour. A careful study of the biblical usage of the word *suffer* shows that the word often means *"to allow"* (*Exodus 12:23; Mark 10:14*). In other words, a Christian suffers, at least in this context, when he allows the Saviour the privilege of controlling the Christian's life. As to the contrasting word *deny*, a careful study will prove that the meaning is often associated with withholding something needed, desired, or requested, or refusal to allow something (*1 Kings 2:16; Proverbs 30:7*).

The conclusive teaching is that faithfulness yields reward while unfaithfulness causes a loss of reward. A yielded Christian will be rewarded with an opportunity to reign over varying regions in the millennial Kingdom. On the other hand, Christians who refuse to allow the Lord the opportunity to reign in their lives while on earth will be refused the privilege of authority in the earthly Kingdom. In short, suffer (allow) the Lord to reign in your life today and He will suffer (allow) you to reign in His Kingdom. Refuse His right in your life today and He will refuse you the opportunity to reign in His Kingdom. Regardless of varying levels of authority within the Kingdom, ALL CHRISTIANS WILL BE PRESENT AND CONTENT WHEN THE LORD ESTABLISHES HIS MILLENNIAL KINGDOM!

> It should, therefore, be no surprise that our Blessed Hope and those blessed words of *comfort* are under extreme attack today.

Words of Comfort

The message of the Lord's Second Coming (aka Christ's Second Advent) is certainly one of hope but is also mixed with ominous warnings, admonitions, and fears. On the other hand, the message of the Church's deliverance at the Rapture is solely one of *comfort*.

> *1 Thessalonians 4:17 Then we which are alive and remain shall be caught up together with them in the clouds, to meet the Lord in the air: **and so shall we ever be with the Lord.** 18 **Wherefore comfort one another with these words.***

When Christ returns for the Church, our bodies will be fashioned like unto His glorious body. We will sail through the air leaving this old world behind to be met—not simply by an angel, but by Christ Himself. We will be transported to our Heavenly destination and face the Judgment Seat of Christ. At the conclusion of Daniel's Seventieth Week, we will return with Christ from Heaven as part of His armies *(Revelation 19:11, 14)* as joint-heirs to establish His earthly and millennial Kingdom. It is easy to understand why Paul admonished believers to constantly rehearse the message of the Blessed Hope. It should, therefore, be no surprise that our Blessed Hope and those blessed words of *comfort* are under extreme attack today. No matter the vociferousness of the attack, Christians must remain vigilant and steadfast.

> In short, suffer (allow) the Lord to reign in your life today and He will suffer (allow) you to reign in His Kingdom.

6

Contrasting the Day of the Lord

First Thessalonians Chapter 5

Missing or ignoring the true context of First Thessalonians chapter 5 has caused many Bible teachers to make unscriptural and false assumptions. Some well-meaning teachers criticize the chapter divisions stating that chapter 5 would more easily assimilate the thoughts of chapter 4 but for the "unfortunate" chapter division. However, the actual context of both chapters reflects a shift from chapter 4 rather than a continuation of its thoughts and teachings. Any argument concerning the chapter divisions serves as a smoke screen that effectively sidetracks the student's focus.

Again, while every chapter in First and Second Thessalonians references the Rapture, four of the chapters also either allude to or specifically address Daniel's Seventieth Week or the coming Day of the Lord. The first chapter to mention the Day of the Lord by name occurs in First Thessalonians chapter 5.

While most Bible teachers appropriately teach that First Thessalonians chapter 4 gives an extensive account of the Rapture, the chief disagreement surrounds the various views concerning the timing of the Rapture. The most commonly held positions are as follows:

1. **The Pre-Tribulation Rapture:** The belief that the Rapture of the Church occurs before the seven-year Tribulation (or any part of Daniel's Seventieth Week) begins; Note: This is the position held by the authors of this work.

2. **The Mid-Tribulation Rapture:** The belief that the Rapture of the Church occurs somewhere in the midst of the seven-year Tribulation, presumably at the midpoint.

3. **The Pre-Wrath Rapture:** The belief that the Church will go through a good portion of the seven-year Tribulation but will be raptured out just prior to a time of God's wrath occurring either toward the end of the Tribulation or just after the conclusion of the Tribulation. Note: While we would agree that the Church will be raptured out prior to the outpouring of wrath, we would consider the entire Tribulation to be a time of God's wrath (either directly or indirectly through Satan and his henchmen).[1]

4. **The Post-Tribulation Rapture:** The belief that the Rapture of the Church occurs after the seven-year Tribulation. The Church is raptured to the clouds only to turn around to come to earth.

The doctrinal disparities found within these four broad categories tend to further heighten an already confused audience. For example, there are some Pre-tribulation teachers who inaccurately believe that Christians will see and recognize the Antichrist prior to the Church's departure, while others rightfully reject this non-scriptural position. (Note: This will be discussed in Second Thessalonians chapter 2.) There also exists varying viewpoints among both Pre-wrath and Post-tribulation believers concerning the timing of shifts away from man's wrath (or Satan's wrath) to the time of God's wrath. Every contrived distinction simply allows unscriptural positions to fester, flourish, and confuse.

---

[1] Those who claim that God's wrath does not begin until the opening of the 6th seal *(Revelation 6:12)* miss the fact that it is Jesus Christ, God the Son, who prevails to loose all seven seals.

*Revelation 5:5 And one of the elders saith unto me, Weep not: behold, **the Lion of the tribe of Juda,** the Root of David, hath **prevailed** to open the book, and **to loose the seven seals** thereof.*

Again, it is the Lamb who opens the seven seals beginning in *Revelation 6:1.*

*Revelation 5:8 And when he had taken the book, the four beasts and four and twenty elders fell down before **the Lamb,** having every one of them harps, and golden vials full of odours, which are the prayers of saints.*

*Revelation 5:9 And they sung a new song, saying, Thou art worthy to take the book, and **to open the seals** thereof: for thou wast slain, and hast redeemed us to God by thy blood out of every kindred, and tongue, and people, and nation;*

Indiscriminately attaching First Thessalonians chapter 4 with chapter 5 reveals one of the most egregious eschatological errors. Those who erroneously place the Rapture's timing within or after the Tribulation period consistently fail to distinguish the proper division between these two subjects. Yet, the shift from one chapter to the next is unmistakable for those who simply read the text within God's intended context.

"BUT" It's Just a Coordinating Conjunction

Reading the Bible with preconceived thoughts or ideas frequently causes the reader to misread a passage to make it say what he thinks it says in order to align with a particular doctrinal system. We may even subconsciously modify, add, or remove a word when we recite a passage in order to make it better say what we think it should say. However, a true Bible believer will guard against such vulnerabilities and will repent when such habits appear in his own thoughts or speech.

> Reading the Bible with preconceived thoughts or ideas frequently causes the reader to misread a passage to make it say what he thinks it says in order to align with a particular doctrinal system.

For a case in point, some confusion in end-times doctrine comes by modifying or ignoring the first word of 1 Thessalonians chapter 5. A common practice is to simply modify the word *but* to be the word *and*. This change may seem insignificant but it assimilates two chapters or contexts rather than recognizing the coordinating conjunction for the particular purpose it serves. Paul used this coordinating conjunction (as he did in verses 4 and 8) to contrast two opposing applications.

While the coordinating conjunction *and* would serve to tie together two similar or connecting thoughts or ideas, the coordinating conjunction *but* in context is used to introduce a statement that contrasts the previously addressed thought or idea. In this case, chapter 4 offers details of the Rapture, **BUT** chapter 5 delves into matters concerning the *"day of the Lord."*

> *1 Thessalonians 5:1 But of the times and the seasons, brethren, ye have no need that I write unto you. 2 For yourselves know perfectly that **the day of the Lord** so cometh as a **thief** in the night.*

If this is not bothersome, perhaps you too are somewhat confused regarding the Day of the Lord. This often occurs when people fail to recognize that the Day of the Lord **IS NOT** the Day of Christ *(Philippians 1:10; Philippians 2:16; 2 Thessalonians 2:2)*. Additionally, the Day of the Lord **IS NOT**: (1) the Day of our Lord Jesus Christ *(1 Corinthians 1:8)*, or (2) the Day of the Lord Jesus *(1 Corinthians 5:5; 2 Corinthians 1:14)*, or (3) the Day of Jesus Christ *(Philippians 1:6)*, or even (4) the Lord's day *(Revelation 1:10)*. The first three reference an event (which will be discussed later in this work) that occurs in conjunction with the Rapture of the Church. The DAY OF THE LORD, however, DOES NOT OCCUR IN CONJUNCTION WITH THE RAPTURE OF THE CHURCH! They are two separate events—with approximately seven years separating the two.

What Is the Day of the Lord?

The Day of the Lord is an event predominately addressed in the Old Testament. However, it is mentioned by name in three New Testament passages. Contextually, these New Testament references offer tremendous insight on the timing and circumstances of the Day of the Lord. Based upon a careful reading of Second Peter chapter 3, the Day of the Lord lasts 1,000 years *(2 Peter 3:8)*. This period is introduced with signs *(Acts 2:20; Joel 2:31)* just prior to the Lord's Second Advent and ends with the burning up of the present heaven and earth *(2 Peter 3:10)*.

Much like the Hebrew day (made up of evening and morning), spiritually speaking the Day of the Lord begins with night. It is a time of darkness rather than light *(Amos 5:18, 20)*. It begins with destruction *(Isaiah 13:6)* based upon God's wrath and fierce anger *(Isaiah 13:9)* and is in response to the controversy of Zion *(Isaiah 34:8)*. This Day commences with the outpouring of God's vengeance upon His adversaries *(Jeremiah 46:10)*. Though this night of suffering may seem long to those who endure it, God's wrath swiftly gives way to the rising of the Sun of righteousness (the Lord Jesus Christ) with healing in His wings *(Malachi 4:2)*.

All things considered, the Day of the Lord holds much more light and

> [The Day of the Lord] commences with the outpouring of God's vengeance upon His adversaries *(Jeremiah 46:10)*… It is a Day when the Lord is "in charge" on earth.

hope for Israel than despair. Though it opens with God's wrath, it swiftly moves to the Lord's deliverance and the establishment of His earthly and millennial Kingdom. It is a Day when the Lord is "in charge" on earth. He is the judge, the king, the prophet, and the priest.

Children of the Day Versus Children of the Night

Not only does the onset of the fifth chapter of First Thessalonians make a notable shift in context as it pertains to future events (from the Rapture in chapter 4 to Day of the Lord in chapter 5), but it also identifies a notable shift in applicable people groups. The recipients of the epistle of First Thessalonians had no need that Paul write to them concerning the Day of the Lord—the same people Paul warned that he *"would not have to be ignorant" (1 Thessalonians 4:13)* concerning the Rapture. However, chapter 5 **indirectly** addresses another group of people that desperately needed to understand Paul's writing concerning the Day of the Lord. Paul refers to them as those who are *"of the night"* or *"of darkness" (1 Thessalonians 5:5)*. Throughout chapter 5, Paul directly addresses the saved in the first person ("you") and refers to those of the night as "they" (who are the lost). It is important to realize that the saved are directly addressed while the lost are only indirectly addressed.

According to Paul *(1 Thessalonians 5:2)*, there was no need for Christians to know about the issues reflected in the early verses of this chapter. Instead, these *"times and . . . seasons"* applied to a *future time* involving a *different group of people*. According to *Acts 1:7*, the times and seasons directly correlate to the establishment of Israel's future Kingdom *(Acts 1:6)*.

> *Acts 1:7 And he said unto them, **It is not for you to know the times or the seasons**, which the Father hath put in his own power.*

Though New Testament saints will take part in the Day of the Lord, it will be in a much different role than that of the Jews or of unsaved Gentiles. We will return with the Lord Jesus as He comes to establish His Kingdom. We will participate (with some believers reigning) in His millennial reign. We will certainly take part in the Day of the Lord, but *"that day"* will not *"overtake"* us *"as a thief" (1 Thessalonians 5:4)*.

The Pronoun Distinctions

The Bible is unlike any other piece of literature. When reading most literary works, the studious reader might be able to skim select paragraphs, sentences, or words and still comprehend the meaning of the literary work. As it pertains to scripture, the failure to carefully observe each word could lead to the acceptance of false doctrine or even heresy. This chapter serves as a great case in point.

In First Thessalonians chapter 5, pronouns play a particularly important role in distinguishing between those who need not be ignorant concerning the Rapture of chapter 4 and those who need not be ignorant concerning the Day of the Lord of chapter 5. According to Paul, the *"day of the Lord"* (*1 Thessalonians 5:2*) pertains to the *"they," "them,"* or *"others"* of verses 3, 6, and 7, but not to the *"ye," "you," "yourselves," "us,"* or *"we"* of verses 1-2, 4-6, and 8-11. The whole context of the discussion is directed to Christians but also indirectly references those ("they") who are not saved. Here is an example of the contrast simply based upon the distinguishing pronouns found in verse 3 versus the pronouns found in verse 4.

> The whole context of the discussion [in First Thessalonians chapter 5] is directed to Christians but also indirectly references those ("they") who are not saved.

> *1 Thessalonians 5:3 For when **they** shall say, Peace and safety; then sudden destruction cometh upon **them**, as travail upon a woman with child; and **they** shall not escape. 4 **But ye, brethren**, are not in darkness, that **that day** (the Day of the Lord) should overtake **you** as a **thief**.*

The Day of the Lord **cannot** *"overtake"* any Christian since Christians are not in darkness and the Day of the Lord comes upon those in darkness. Why are Christians *not* in darkness—for the simple reason that Christians are the Children of Light! What if some Christian stops living like a child of light? Does he cease being one of the children of light? No, this individual is simply spiritually sleeping.

It is important to emphasize that this chapter as the others **always** directly addresses the saved (the "you" of the passage), but repeatedly varies its focus from those in darkness (*they* and *them*) to the *brethren* (or *ye*). Who proclaims *"Peace and safety"*? Who suffers sudden destruction? Who does not escape this destruction? In each case, it is unmistakably *not* the brethren. It is the "them" mentioned—it is the lost.

Interestingly, verse 4 begins with the same coordinating conjunction (*but*) as verse 1 which further emphasizes how this word contrasts two opposing groups in verse 4 or viewpoints in verse 1. In this case, the brethren (ye/you) are contrasted with those in the coming Tribulation (they/them). Verses 5 and 6 remain focused upon the believers (*ye, we, and us*).

> *1 Thessalonians 5:5 Ye are all the children of light, and the children of the day: **we** are not of the night, nor of darkness. 6 Therefore let **us** not sleep, as do others; but let **us** watch and be sober.*

Those who overlook or ignore the intended contrast between the two groups of chapter 5 miss the entire import of what is taught. Who is it that needs to be concerned with the thief, the darkness, and the Day of the Lord? It is certainly not the children of light! Our responsibility is to remain alert no matter the promises of God. Those teachers who disregard the distinctive divisions between these two groups are the same ones who fail to account for the difference between the Rapture of the Church and Jesus Christ returning to the Mount of Olives at the Second Coming.

Verse 7 again shifts the focus from *us* (the children of the day—the saved) to *they* (the children of the night—the lost). In the next verse, the Bible again incorporates the coordinating conjunction (*but*) in order to identify a shift back from *they* (*1 Thessalonians 5:7*) to *us* (*1 Thessalonians 5:8*). These distinctions are purposeful, necessary, and imperative for a proper understanding.[2]

> Those who overlook or ignore the intended contrast between the two groups of chapter 5 miss the entire import of what is taught.

> *1 Thessalonians 5:7 For **they** that sleep sleep in the night; and **they** that be drunken are drunken in the night. 8 But let **us, who are of the day,** be sober, putting on the breastplate of faith and love; and for **an helmet, the hope of salvation.***

Once again, the people in verse 7 are contrasted with those in verse 8, similar to how the primary event covered in chapter 4 is contrasted with the onset of chapter 5. The next three verses of chapter 5 (verses 9

---

[2] Note: Proverbs chapter 10 offers another excellent example of how the word but is used to highlight contrasts. For instance, verses 1-14 each use "but" to show contrast and then verses 15-16 use the colon to show contrast without the word "but."

through 11) continue addressing the group of verse 8 (the children of the day or of the light—the saved).

> *1 Thessalonians 5:9 For God hath not appointed **us** to wrath, but to obtain salvation by our Lord Jesus Christ, 10 Who died for **us**, that, whether we wake or sleep, **we** should live together with him. 11 Wherefore comfort **yourselves** together, and edify one another, even as also **ye** do.*

This passage verifies the fact that the Church will not remain on earth for any part of Daniel's Seventieth Week. The Church will leave at the Rapture and be supernaturally spared from any future wrath (including Daniel's Seventieth Week and the Day of the Lord). Instead of wrath, we have *the hope of salvation (1 Thessalonians 5:8).* This hope is the Blessed Hope *(Titus 2:13)* and this salvation is a physical deliverance which involves living *together with him (1 Thessalonians 5:10).* This salvation comes by our Lord Jesus Christ and is the salvation said to be *"nearer than when we believed."*

> *Romans 13:11 And that, knowing the time, that now it is high time to **awake out of sleep: for now is our salvation nearer than when we believed.***

Chapter 5: Consider the Pronouns (written to the brethren)	
1 Thessalonians 5:1 (the brethren)	"But of the times and the seasons, brethren, ye have no need that I write unto you."
1 Thessalonians 5:2 (the brethren)	"For yourselves know perfectly that the day of the Lord so cometh as a thief in the night."
1 Thessalonians 5:3 (the Lost)	"For when they shall say, Peace and safety; then sudden destruction cometh upon them, as travail upon a woman with child; and they shall not escape."
1 Thessalonians 5:4 (the brethren)	"But ye, brethren, are not in darkness, that that day should overtake you as a thief."
1 Thessalonians 5:5 (the brethren)	"Ye are all the children of light, and the children of the day: we are not of the night, nor of darkness."
1 Thessalonians 5:6 (the brethren)	"Therefore let us not sleep, as do others; but let us watch and be sober."
1 Thessalonians 5:7 (the Lost)	"For they that sleep sleep in the night; and they that be drunken are drunken in the night."
	[Chart 1.51]

Chapter 5: Consider the Pronouns (written to the brethren)	
1 Thessalonians 5:8 (the brethren)	"But let us, who are of the day, be sober, putting on the breastplate of faith and love; and for an helmet, the hope of salvation."
1 Thessalonians 5:9 (the brethren)	"For God hath not appointed us to wrath, but to obtain salvation by our Lord Jesus Christ,"
1 Thessalonians 5:10 (the brethren)	"Who died for us, that, whether we wake or sleep, we should live together with him."
1 Thessalonians 5:11 (the brethren)	"Wherefore comfort yourselves together, and edify one another, even as also ye do."
1 Thessalonians 5:23 (the brethren)	"And the very God of peace sanctify you wholly; and I pray God your whole spirit and soul and body be preserved blameless unto the coming of our Lord Jesus Christ."
	[Chart 1.51]

The Church's deliverance from Daniel's Seventieth Week does not mean that the believers' tribulations will not continue to escalate as we see the Day approaching. However, the same group of brethren comforted in chapter 4 are again comforted in chapter 5 (the *us* and not the *them* in the context). The Church will not have to endure one millisecond of Jacob's Trouble nor any part of Daniel's Seventieth Week! This also indicates that the Church will not have to endure one millisecond of God's wrath! Instead, we will enjoy the salvation (physical deliverance of our bodies—aka the Adoption) granted by the Lord Jesus Christ and so shall we ever be with the Lord. God offers comfort to those willing to take God's word at face value!!!!

> The Church's deliverance from Daniel's Seventieth Week does not mean that the believers' tribulations will not continue to escalate as we see the Day approaching.

Blessed Hope of Corinthians

1 Corinthians 15:51 Behold, I shew you a mystery; We shall not all sleep, but we shall all be changed,

52 In a moment, in the twinkling of an eye, at the last trump: for the trumpet shall sound, and the dead shall be raised incorruptible, and we shall be changed.

53 For this corruptible must put on incorruption, and this mortal must put on immortality.

54 So when this corruptible shall have put on incorruption, and this mortal shall have put on immortality, then shall be brought to pass the saying that is written, Death is swallowed up in victory.

55 O death, where is thy sting? O grave, where is thy victory?

56 The sting of death is sin; and the strength of sin is the law.

57 But thanks be to God, which giveth us the victory through our Lord Jesus Christ.

58 Therefore, my beloved brethren, be ye stedfast, unmoveable, always abounding in the work of the Lord, forasmuch as ye know that your labour is not in vain in the Lord.

7

Why This Second Epistle?

Second Thessalonians

Why did God compel Paul to address two epistles to the believers at Corinth and Thessalonica while addressing only one epistle each to the believers at Rome, Colosse, Ephesus, Philippi and Galatia? We know the *Corinthians* received a second epistle, at least in part, due to their struggles with carnality. The *Thessalonians*, however, received their second epistle, at least in part, to clear up confusion introduced in their midst concerning the end-times' events and their scenario and sequence.

> The *Thessalonians*, however, received their second epistle, at least in part, to clear up confusion introduced in their midst concerning the end-times' events and their scenario and sequence.

Based upon the textual indicators found within Second Thessalonians, it is quite clear that some unbelievers (likely Jewish) convinced the saints that the Rapture/resurrection had passed and they had been left behind. With that in mind, this epistle was written with a twofold purpose: (1) encouraging the saints to remember and hold fast those things which Paul had spoken to them,

> *2 Thessalonians 2:5 Remember ye not, that, when I was yet with you, **I told you these things**?*

and (2) to encourage the saints to rest with Paul knowing that God would later recompense tribulation to those causing the trouble.

*2 Thessalonians 1:6 Seeing it is a righteous thing with **God** to **recompense tribulation to them that trouble you;** 7 And to you who are troubled rest with us, **when the Lord Jesus shall be revealed from heaven with his mighty angels,***

In the case of the Thessalonian believers, their most disturbing trouble resulted from a letter written, delivered, and disseminated among the believers. The letter was written by those hoping to destroy the great hope exhibited by the Thessalonians.

This letter might not have been as effective had it not been forged to indicate that it came from the apostle Paul *(2 Thessalonians 2:2)*. Furthermore, it is likely that the misrepresentations of truth found in this letter were spreading like wildfire through the disorderly brethren. These particular brethren were not working, but traveled from one house to the next spreading false traditions contrary to those received from Paul.

*2 Thessalonians 3:6 Now we command you, brethren, in the name of our Lord Jesus Christ, that ye **withdraw yourselves from every brother that walketh disorderly,** and not after the tradition which he received of us.*

*2 Thessalonians 3:11 For we hear that there are some which walk among you **disorderly,** working not at all, but are **busybodies.***

The Thessalonians' hope in the Blessed Hope *(Titus 2:13)* was in peril should things not be corrected. The saints were shaken in mind and this second epistle was written to clear up the resulting confusion. In this letter, Paul provided additional insight into end-time events and admonished believers to renew their patience in waiting for Christ *(2 Thessalonians 3:5)*.

Paul provided additional insight into end-time events and admonished believers to renew their patience in waiting for Christ *(2 Thessalonians 3:5)*. Paul even went so far as to let believers know the key to assigning his authorship to any letter.

*2 Thessalonians 3:17 The salutation of Paul with mine own hand, **which is the token in every epistle:** so I write. 18 The grace of our Lord Jesus Christ be with you all. Amen.*

8

Parenthetical Passages

Second Thessalonians Chapter 1

Those who exalt God's word to its rightful place of supremacy understand that the context of any passage is of utmost importance. This means that no passage or thought can be properly understood independent of surrounding passages or thoughts.[1] Part of understanding the context of a passage is to consider sentence structure. This is especially true when considering prophetic truths.

Consider these facts about Second Thessalonians chapter 1 which will reveal the complexity of the sentence structure within the chapter. This chapter contains 28.5% of the words found in the entire three chapter epistle (291 of 1,022), and 25.5% of the verses (12 of the 47); however, it *only* contains 10% of the sentences (3 of the 30). These facts demonstrate that the first chapter contains only one tenth of the sentences, but includes over one fourth of the words and verses. Needless to say, the sentences in chapter 1 are lengthy with one sentence covering over one half of all the verses within the chapter.

> Part of understanding the context of a passage is to consider sentence structure. This is especially true when considering prophetic truths.

This one lengthy sentence in Second Thessalonians chapter one holds particular importance as it pertains to prophecy. It covers seven verses beginning in *2 Thessalonians 1:3* and ending in *2 Thessalonians*

---

[1] perhaps with the exception of Proverbs

1:10. This sentence structure is by no means accidental. The sentence contains 195 words, 11 commas, 3 semicolons, 3 colons, 2 parentheses, and 1 period! While details may seem dull or tedious, it must be remembered that we are called to be *workmen* as it pertains to Bible study *(2 Timothy 2:15)*.

Misunderstanding the complexities of Bible sentence structure has led to many false assumptions regarding the timing and meaning of certain Bible events. In fact, many teachers of false doctrines are also lackadaisical grammarians who tend to force their interpretative doctrines upon innocent Christians sincerely desiring to know the truth. This is particularly true concerning our subject passage!

The three semicolons found in Second Thessalonians chapter 1 are each followed by a further explanation of the statements preceding. Two of the three phrases ending with the semicolons are followed (directly or indirectly) by the word *when (2 Thessalonians 1:6-7, 9-10)*. In other words, each of the first statements will be fulfilled in the future *when* the second statement happens (see the table below). Read each of these statements together from left to right in order to understand their timing and sequence.

This Shall Happen:	When	This Happens:
"it is a righteous thing with God to recompense tribulation to them that trouble you;" *(2 Thessalonians 1:6)*	when	*"the Lord Jesus shall be revealed from heaven with his mighty angels" (2 Thessalonians 1:7)*
"Who shall be punished with everlasting destruction" *(2 Thessalonians 1:9)*	When	*"he shall come to be glorified in his saints, and to be admired in all them that believe" (2 Thessalonians 1:10)*

As Paul began his second letter to the Thessalonians, he admonished them that no matter the extent of the troubles faced, they were to *rest* secure with him. Unfortunately, many Pre-wrath teachers (those teaching that the Church will go through the Tribulation and leave just prior to the onset of God's wrath) are again guilty of superficial Bible study and interpretation. They look at the first word in the second clause of verse 7 beginning with *"when"* to incorrectly teach that the *rest* mentioned will not take place until the Lord returns at the Second Coming! This faulty understanding creates its own set of issues. The truth can be ascertained only by considering the tense of each clause.

> **2 Thessalonians 1:6** *Seeing it is a righteous thing with God to recompense tribulation (<u>future</u>) to them that trouble you (<u>present</u>); 7* ***And to you who are troubled*** *(<u>present</u>)* ***rest with us*** *(<u>present</u>), when the Lord Jesus shall be revealed from heaven with his mighty angels (<u>future</u>),*

Simply put, the context of the passage advises believers to *rest* (present tense) who are *troubled* (present tense) since God will recompense (future tense) those who are *presently* troubling His saints. Those who misinterpret the passage claim that Christians are only going to rest or find relief sometime in the future. This is a false assumption and pretense!

The Bible clearly says that God's *recompense* **(2 Thessalonians 1:6)** will take place WHEN the Lord Jesus shall be revealed from Heaven with His mighty angels **(2 Thessalonians 1:7)**. The wicked shall be punished with everlasting destruction **(2 Thessalonians 1:9)** WHEN the Lord shall come to be glorified in His saints **(2 Thessalonians 1:10)**. Because of these prophetic promises, the saints should no longer be troubled, but should *"rest with us"* **(2 Thessalonians 1:7)**. The "us" are easily identified in the context as Paul, Silvanus, and Timotheus **(2 Thessalonians 1:1)**.

> Why do Pre-wrath and Post-tribulationists falsely teach the believer's rest or relief does not take place until Christ returns?

Why do Pre-wrath and Post-tribulationists falsely teach the believer's rest or relief does not take place until Christ returns? This misinterpretation helps to bolster their erroneous teachings concerning the timing of the Rapture. Yet, even a superficial application of English language principles permits the reader to understand how the Bible expresses a break in thought. When Bible teachers ignore these breaks, passages can be skewed to teach false doctrine. This is especially true of those who deem punctuation unimportant, irrelevant, or of no use. In **2 Thessalonians 1:7**, the punctuation breaks the thought into two independent clauses with the first clause serving as a parenthetical thought. These parenthetical phrases are found throughout scripture.[2]

Christians do not have to wait for Christ's return to *rest*. We can now rest knowing that God WILL repay all those who do us wrong *(Romans 12:19)*. *2 Thessalonians 1:5-6* provides the context of the parenthetical thought found in verse 7 while verse 10 offers a second parenthetical thought as a further example of this grammatical tool, this time separated by parentheses.

> *2 Thessalonians 1:5 Which is a manifest token of the righteous judgment of God, that ye may be counted worthy of the kingdom of God, for which **ye** also **suffer:** 6 Seeing it is a righteous thing with **God to recompense tribulation to them that trouble you**; 7 And to you who are troubled rest with us, **when the Lord Jesus shall be revealed from heaven** with his mighty angels, 8 In flaming fire **taking vengeance** on them that know not God, and that obey not the gospel of our Lord Jesus Christ: 9 **Who shall be punished** with everlasting destruction from the presence of the Lord, and from the glory of his power; 10 When he shall come to be glorified in his saints, and to be admired in all them that believe **(because our testimony among you was believed)** in that day.*

The second phrase of verse 7, *"when the Lord Jesus shall be revealed from heaven,"* completes the statement and offers the timing of *"God to recompense tribulation to them that trouble you."* The parenthetical portion (*"And to you who are troubled rest with us"*) splits the complete thought. God always provides ample proof for those willing to study and provides the spiritual impediment for those who desire to force their private interpretations. Verse 10 offers further proof of the Bible's design

---

[2] The authors are acutely aware of the fact that the original Greek manuscripts had no punctuation. These manuscripts were also written in all caps with no spaces! In addition, the Hebrew did not even have any vowels. English has punctuation, spaces, and includes vowels for good reason. These grammatical elements are what give English meaning and offer the reader understanding. For instance, consider the impact of removing or ignoring the punctuation in *Luke 23:32.* **Without punctuation:** *(And there were also **two other malefactors** led with him to be put to death);* **with the correct punctuation:** *And there were also **two other, malefactors,** led with him to be put to death.* Greek and Hebrew did not require punctuation; English certainly does. To claim that what was sufficient for the Greek and Hebrew is adequate for the English is to make Jesus a sinner. Those claiming as much have no concept of what it takes to translate from one language into another.

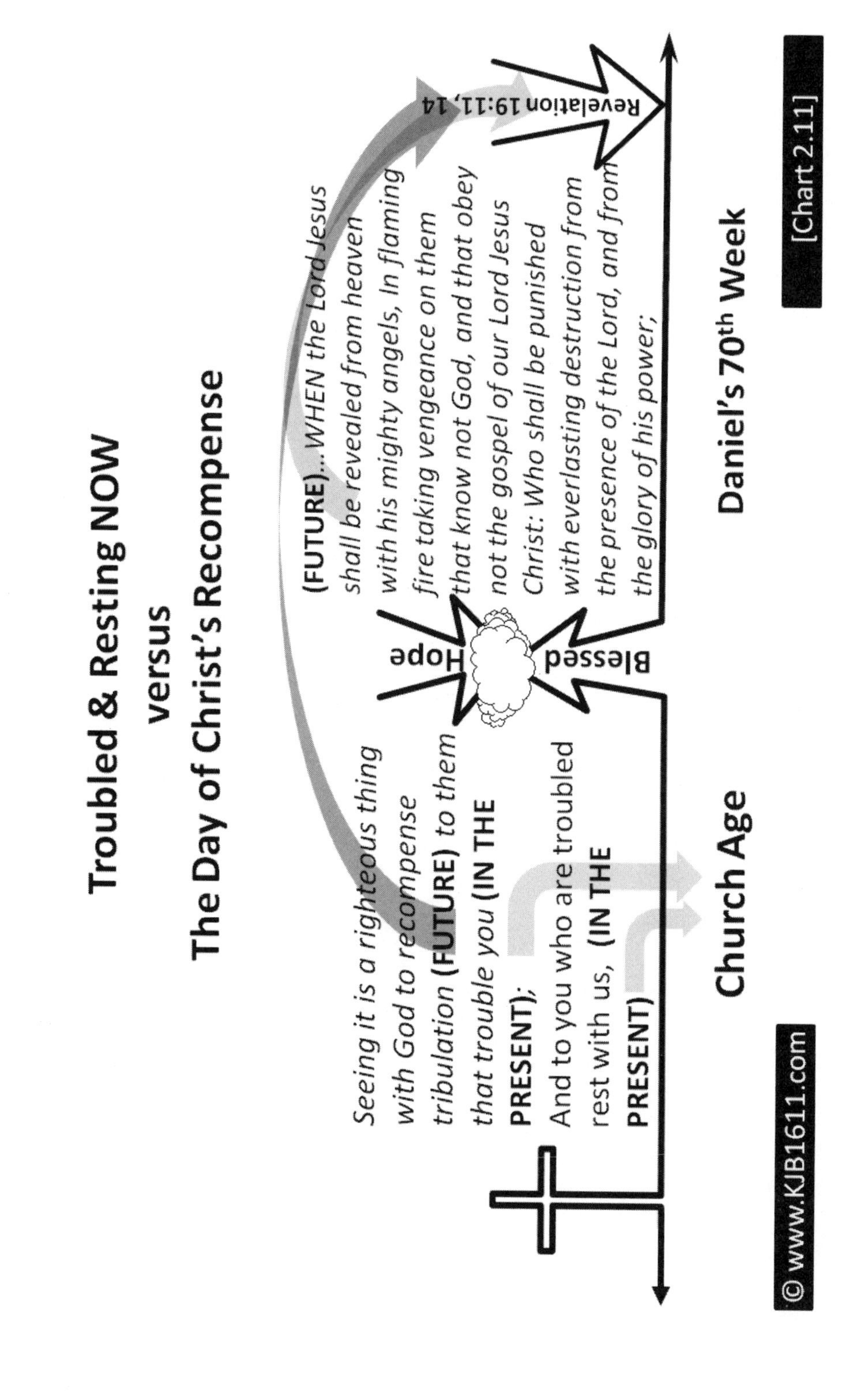
Troubled & Resting NOW
versus
The Day of Christ's Recompense
Seeing it is a righteous thing with God to recompense tribulation (FUTURE) to them that trouble you (IN THE PRESENT);
And to you who are troubled rest with us, (IN THE PRESENT)
Blessed Hope
(FUTURE)...WHEN the Lord Jesus shall be revealed from heaven with his mighty angels, In flaming fire taking vengeance on them that know not God, and that obey not the gospel of our Lord Jesus Christ: Who shall be punished with everlasting destruction from the presence of the Lord, and from the glory of his power;
Revelation 19:11, 14
Church Age
Daniel's 70th Week
© www.KJB1611.com
[Chart 2.11]

as it contains another example of a parenthetical thought with this instance set off by a set of parentheses *"(because our...believed)."*

Those who are troubled can rest assured that God will recompense (or repay) tribulation to those who trouble them. This recompense will take place when the Lord is revealed to take out His vengeance upon a rebellious world. Some of the passages which help us to understand how God's recompense takes place would be **Romans 12:19, Deuteronomy 32:35, Ruth 2:12, Nahum 1:2**, and...

> **Deuteronomy 7:9** *Know therefore that **the LORD thy God,** he is God, the faithful God, which keepeth covenant and mercy with them that love him and keep his commandments to a thousand generations; 10 And **repayeth them that hate him to their face,** to destroy them: he will not be slack to him that hateth him, **he will repay him to his face.***

God is going to repay the lost! Fortunately, Christians are never told that they must wait until Christ returns to rest but can presently *rest* in and on His divine promises.[3]

---

[3] There are many other examples of the importance of the Bible's grammatical features. However, First Timothy contains another excellent example for anyone that might remain unconvinced concerning God's grammatical methodology. A parenthetical expression can be removed from a sentence and the primary flow of the sentence remains intact without the additional thought(s) that are parenthetically added into the passage. In the next example, verse 11 completes the thought of verse 8 with verses 9 and 10 added parenthetically (bookended by two semicolons). Read all four verses together and then read only verses 8 and 11 together to see how to understand this scriptural method.

1 Timothy 1:8 But we know that the law is good, if a man use it lawfully;

9 Knowing this, that the law is not made for a righteous man, but for the lawless and disobedient, for the ungodly and for sinners, for unholy and profane, for murderers of fathers and murderers of mothers, for manslayers, 10 For whoremongers, for them that defile themselves with mankind, for menstealers, for liars, for perjured persons, and if there be any other thing that is contrary to sound doctrine;

11 According to the glorious gospel of the blessed God, which was committed to my trust.

As you can see, Paul uses a similar technique in First Timothy as our subject passage from Second Thessalonians chapter 1. It simply takes work to understand the depths and riches of scripture. In fact, God allowed the Bible to be written in such

As further proof *against* the teaching that there is no rest for God's children until the Second Coming *(Revelation 19:11)*, consider Revelation chapter 6. The Bible plainly teaches that there are those who will be resting prior to the Second Coming and God's administered vengeance.

> *Revelation 6:9 And when he had opened the **fifth seal**, I saw under the altar the souls of them that were slain for the word of God, and for the testimony which they held: 10 And they cried with a loud voice, saying, How long, O Lord, holy and true, dost thou not judge and avenge our blood on them that dwell on the earth? 11 And white robes were given unto every one of them; and it was said unto them, that **they should rest** yet for a little season, until their fellowservants also and their brethren, that should be killed as they were, should be fulfilled.*

The Bible plainly points to a scene in Heaven at the opening of the fifth seal. This seal shows the souls of the saints in Heaven who have been killed during the Tribulation. These saints are instructed to *rest* long before the Second Coming takes place. This passage from Revelation further disproves any teaching that *2 Thessalonians 1:7* was meant by God to imply that no one will experience any *rest*

> If scripture contradicts any proclaimed "truth," this makes the teaching a *private interpretation.*

prior to Christ's return to earth to mete out His vengeance. This point also serves as proof that preachers must preach and teachers must declare *all the counsel of God (Acts 20:27)*. If scripture contradicts any proclaimed "truth," this makes the teaching a *private interpretation.*

> *2 Peter 1:20 Knowing this first, that no prophecy of the scripture is of any **private interpretation.***

Context Answers the Critics

Some critics of Pre-tribulation Rapture teachers falsely claim that any Pre-tribulation Rapture teaching is simply an escapist doctrine. In other words, those who believe that the Church will be raptured prior to the Tribulation period teach this because they want to escape the horrors prophesied to take place on earth during Daniel's Seventieth Week. They

a way that if a person wishes to twist any teaching toward a particular preconceived angle, he could easily do so, both innocently and ignorantly *(2 Peter 3:15-16).*

want to escape persecution. This argument has no scriptural or factual support whatsoever because suffering *in this life* plays a significant role in the Christian's way of life throughout time.

Recall the very long sentence found in chapter 1 begins in verse 3. It is important to take note of the full context of the teaching. Paul began, from verse 3 through the first part of verse 4, by commending the believers' charity, patience, and faith.

> *2 Thessalonians 1:3 We are bound to thank God always for you, brethren, as it is meet, because that your **faith** groweth exceedingly, and the **charity** of every one of you all toward each other aboundeth; 4 So that we ourselves glory in you in the churches of God for your **patience** and **faith...***

As Paul commended these laudable qualities, he pointed out that they lived this way in the midst of great adversities.

> *...**in all your persecutions and tribulations** that ye endure: 5 Which is a manifest token of the righteous judgment of God, that ye may be counted worthy of the kingdom of God, **for which ye also suffer:***

Paul commends these believers for their reaction to the persecutions, tribulations, and sufferings. That being said, those who claim teachers of the Pre-tribulation Rapture are simply "escapists" are either extremely misinformed or treacherously deceptive or both. The facts are that the longer the Lord tarries His return, the more persecution, tribulation, and suffering Christians will experience. Bottom line: Each year will see escalating persecution worldwide at varying

> [T]hose who claim teachers of the Pre-tribulation Rapture are simply "escapists" are either extremely misinformed or treacherously deceptive or both.

degrees against all Christians prior to the Pre-tribulation Rapture. The Bible foretells the Church's future on earth as *"evil men and seducers shall wax **worse and worse**" (**2 Timothy 3:13**) "in the last days" (**2 Timothy 3:1**).*

9

The Day of Christ

Second Thessalonians Chapter 2

2 Thessalonians 2:1-2

The Bible contains chapters scattered throughout that impact a teaching so profoundly that they take on the identity of being an authoritative treatise on the particular subject. As it pertains to the Church's departure, the Bible contains three chapters (First Corinthians chapter 15, First Thessalonians chapter 4, and Second Thessalonians chapter 2) which unite to provide a comprehensive narrative of the Church's end-times. The particular role of Second Thessalonians chapter 2 is to identify events both preceding and simultaneously occurring on **the Day of Christ**.

Unfortunately, the facts of this chapter are often misrepresented on both sides of the eschatological spectrum. Those attempting to disprove the Pre-tribulation Rapture treat Second Thessalonians as their decisive argument. Unfortunately, far too many of those who believe in the Pre-tribulation Rapture simply parrot what they have been taught concerning the premise of the chapter. These teachings have further resulted in a wide array of incorrect traditions and teachings. Some men have even changed the scripture to support their version of "the truth." Consequently, the multiplicity of teachings has caused much

> [F]ar too many of those who believe in the Pre-tribulation Rapture simply parrot what they have been taught concerning the premise of the chapter.

confusion *(1 Corinthians 14:33)* and become as howling winds tossing believers to and fro *(Ephesians 4:14).*

Second Thessalonians chapter 2 immediately addresses its audience—*"brethren"* and makes an appeal based upon *"the coming of our Lord Jesus Christ."* The coming referenced is not the Second Coming (when Christ sets His foot upon the earth), but Christ's return for His Church (when we meet Him in the air). This is especially obvious by the reference to *"our gathering together unto him."* The appeal—*"that ye be not soon shaken...or...troubled"* is made possible only through a proper understanding of the factual details of the arrival of *"the mystery of iniquity" (2 Thessalonians 2:7)*—the opposite or antithesis to *"the mystery of godliness" (1 Timothy 3:16).*

The context shows that it became necessary for Paul to make such an appeal to these saints because of a counterfeit letter—one supposedly from him that completely bewildered and confused the believers of Thessalonica. The imposter had written to these believers claiming they were missing the events in Heaven commencing with *"our gathering together unto him* [Christ]." Understanding the first two verses of the chapter lays the groundwork for comprehending the end-time events pertaining to both the Church and the Jews.

> Understanding the first two verses of the chapter lays the groundwork for comprehending the end-time events pertaining to both the Church and the Jews.

> *2 Thessalonians 2:1 Now we beseech you, brethren, by the **coming** of our Lord Jesus Christ, and by **our gathering together** unto him, 2 That ye be not soon shaken in mind, or be troubled, neither by spirit, nor by word, nor by **letter** as from us, as that the **day of Christ** is at hand.*

The Thessalonian saints must have inquired concerning a forged letter that had contradicted what Paul had personally taught them earlier. In his previous discussions with the Thessalonians, Paul clearly expounded to them the Lord's *coming* and the believers' *"gathering together unto him" (1 Thessalonians 4:13-18).* As Paul was accustomed to doing with the saints *(Philippians 3:1)*, he reiterated the truths taught previously both by epistle *(1 Thessalonians 4:13-18)* and by personal communication *(2 Thessalonians 2:5).*

The false letter writer(s) could be a reference to those mentioned by Paul in *2 Timothy 2:17-18* who did not rightly divide the word of truth *(2 Timothy 2:15)*. He says of Hymenaeus and Philetus that they erred—teaching that the resurrection *"is past already."* Their hope-destroying teaching overthrew the faith of some of the believers.

> *2 Timothy 2:18 Who concerning the truth have erred, **saying that the resurrection is past already**; and overthrow the faith of some.*

The Christian's greatest strength involves his faith while the Devil's greatest weapon involves deception *(John 8:44; 2 Corinthians 4:3-4; 2 Corinthians 11:13-15)*! It should come as no surprise that one of the Devil's primary objectives involves attacking the believer's greatest strength (his childlike faith). Historically, Satan's most profound accomplishments have involved planting conflicting information in men's minds and hearts. The greatest

> Satan's most profound accomplishments have involved planting conflicting information in men's minds and hearts.

damage arises when those with an unwavering faith fail to realize that their "faith" is established upon a false and faulty premise.

Hymenaeus and Philetus *(2 Timothy 2:17-18)* achieved Satan's desired outcome by creating a mustard seed of doubt concerning God's truth. These two said the resurrection had already past. They could easily have used the event recorded in the Gospel books to convince believers that the resurrection had already taken place. After Jesus died on the cross, the earth quaked and the rocks were torn apart. The religious leaders most likely tried to blame the earthquake for the tearing of the temple veil. However, what happened three days later concerning the resurrected bodies could not so easily be explained away.

> *Matthew 27:50 Jesus, when he had cried again with a loud voice, yielded up the ghost. 51 And, behold, the veil of the temple was rent in twain from the top to the bottom; and the earth did quake, and the rocks rent; 52 And the graves were opened; and **many bodies of the saints which slept arose**, 53 And **came out of the graves after his resurrection, and went into the holy city, and appeared unto many**.*

After Christ's resurrection, the bodies in the opened graves resurrected and appeared in Jerusalem. This limited resurrection may have been a focal point used by those claiming that the Resurrection and Rapture had already taken place. Those promoting false doctrines (by mouth or by counterfeit epistles) must have had some compelling arguments, otherwise their attacks would not have been so convincing and confusing to the believers. An ineffective lie would not have invoked such a response from the apostle Paul.

Whatever the arguments used, the Thessalonian believers grew increasingly concerned that the Day of Christ was at hand and that they had somehow misunderstood Paul's teachings and missed the Rapture. For this reason, the apostle Paul reached out again to these believers intending to restore their hope in the Blessed Hope.

First, it is imperative to make some distinctions concerning correct biblical terminology. For example, *"the day of Christ"* *(2 Thessalonians 2:2)* must be accurately distinguished from *"the day of the Lord"* *(1 Thessalonians 5:2)*. THEY ARE NOT SYNONYMOUS but refer to two separate and distinct events! As already discussed, *"the day of the Lord"* is approximately, if not exactly, a 1,000 year period of time. The Day of the Lord begins just prior to the Lord's Second Advent and the accompanying wrath. It continues through the millennial Kingdom concluding with the passing away of the heaven and earth *(2 Peter 3:10)*.

"The day of Christ," on the other hand, commences at the Rapture of the Church and includes events that take place in Heaven *(1 Corinthians 3:13; Philippians 1:6, 10; Philippians 2:16)* simultaneous to Daniel's Seventieth Week taking place upon the earth. In fact, here are ten truths about the Day of Christ to consider.

Facts Concerning the Day of Christ	Scriptural Proof
1. God's working within the life of the Christian will continue until that day.	*Philippians 1:6 Being confident of this very thing, that he which hath begun a good work in you will* **perform it until the day of Jesus Christ:**
2. Paul's prayer for the believers was that they would remain faithful until that day.	*Philippians 1:10 That ye may approve things that are excellent; that ye may be sincere and without offence* **till the day of Christ;**

3. Paul desired to rejoice in that day that he had not run or laboured in vain.	*Philippians 2:16 Holding forth the word of life; that I may **rejoice in the day of Christ**, that I have not run in vain, neither laboured in vain.*
4. Christians are to presently live in such a way as to be blameless in that day.	*1 Corinthians 1:7 So that ye come behind in no gift; **waiting for the coming** of our Lord Jesus Christ: 8 Who shall also confirm you unto the end, that ye may be **blameless in the day of our Lord Jesus Christ**.*
5. In that day, each Christian shall stand before the Judgment Seat of Christ (Romans 14:10; 2 Corinthians 5:10).	*1 Corinthians 3:13 Every man's work shall be made manifest: **for the day shall declare it**, because it shall be revealed by fire; and the fire shall try every man's work of what sort it is.*
6. Paul tells of a man whose flesh was turned over to Satan but his spirit was saved in that day.	*1 Corinthians 5:5 To deliver such an one unto Satan for the destruction of the flesh, that the spirit may be saved **in the day of the Lord Jesus**.*
7. In that day, we will rejoice over those believers whom we have affected.	*2 Corinthians 1:14 As also ye have acknowledged us in part, that we are your rejoicing, even as ye also are ours **in the day of the Lord Jesus**.*
8. Paul knew his commitment to the Lord would manifest itself in that day.	*2 Timothy 1:12 For the which cause I also suffer these things: nevertheless I am not ashamed: for I know whom I have believed, and am persuaded that he is able to keep that which I have committed unto him **against that day**.*
9. Paul prayed his fellowservant would find mercy in that day.	*2 Timothy 1:18 The Lord grant unto him that he may find **mercy of the Lord in that day**: and in how many things he ministered unto me at Ephesus, thou knowest very well.*
10. There is a special crown at that day for those who love the Lord's appearing.	*2 Timothy 4:8 Henceforth there is laid up for me a crown of righteousness, which the Lord, the righteous judge, shall give me **at that day**: and not to me only, but unto all them also that love his appearing.*

One can readily ascertain why the Thessalonian believers would be troubled if they suspected the Day of Christ[1] was "at hand" in Heaven

---

[1] **Further Remarks on #6 above** *(1 Corinthians 5:5):* The NIV, ESV, HCSV, etc., along with the Jehovah's Witnesses' New World Translation and the 2010 Catholic New American Bible Revised Edition (NABRD) ignore the majority text and follow the *Vaticanus* reading. Each of these modern versions incorrectly translates *1 Corinthians 5:5* as *"the Day of the Lord"* rather than the *"day of the Lord **Jesus**"* contrary to the overwhelming Greek evidence (last word = ιησου—**Jesus**) and historical support too voluminous to delineate herein (e.g., Tertullian (AD 217), etc.).

and they remained upon the earth. This would mean they had missed the Blessed Hope and the rewards to follow. With this in mind, the apostle Paul sought to comfort the believers. He stressed that the Day of Christ and its associated events were not presently taking place. Instead, believers needed their hearts once again directed *"into the patient waiting for Christ"* *(2 Thessalonians 3:5)*.

A Falling Away First (2 Thessalonians 2:3)

While the Day of Christ is underway *in Heaven*, the Man of Sin will be at work actively deceiving earth's inhabitants. This man will make a covenant with the Jews in the beginning of Daniel's Seventieth Week only to betray them midway through this period, revealing his true nature. For this reason and others, without distinguishing between

Even the context concerning the spirit being saved proves that this is not the judgment upon the earth on the Day of the Lord as described below, but the Rapture of believers to meet the Lord Jesus in the air. This change in these modern versions supplies fodder to some Post-tribulation teachers who want to equate this passage with *the only reference* made by the apostle Paul and the *"sudden destruction"* on the *"day of the Lord"* in *1 Thessalonians 5:2*.

The error is compounded when the ESV, NASV, NIV, HCSV, Catholic Douay-Rheims, Jehovah's Witnesses' New World Translation, etc., also mistranslate *2 Thessalonians 2:2* as the Day of the **Lord** rather than the Day of **Christ** contrary to the overwhelming Greek evidence (last word = χριστου—**Christ**). The Facts: The beginning of the Day of the Lord is not associated with comforting believers (i.e., the Rapture) but with the Lord's vengeance against His enemies *(Isaiah 2:12, 13:6, 13:9, 34:8, 46:10; Lamentations 2:22; Ezekiel 13:5, 30:3; Joel 1:15, 2:1, 2:11, 2:31, 3:14; Amos 5:18, 5:20; Obadiah 15; Zephaniah 1:7, 8, 1:14, 1:18, 2:2, 3; Zechariah 14:1; Malachi 4:5; Acts 2:20; 1 Thessalonians 5:2)*. These passages concerning the onset of the Day of the Lord (when the Lord takes control upon this earth) refer to *destruction, howling, cruel wrath, fierce anger, desolation, vengeance, recompense, day of terrors, the Lord's anger, cloudy day, time of the heathen, alarm trumpets, trembling, great and very terrible day, sun turned into darkness, moon into blood, darkness, day of the Lord's sacrifice, punishment, bitter crying, dreadful day*, and all of this coming as a *thief* upon an unsuspecting, unrepentant world *(Revelation 9:20-21, 16:9-11)*. This surely does not equate to the Day of Christ mentioned in the ten examples above! The Day of the Lord will encompass the Lord's day of vengeance upon His enemies and continue through the Lord's 1,000 year reign upon the earth *(2 Peter 3:10)*, the heavens passing away, and the formation of the new heaven and new earth *(Revelation 21:1)*. Those failing to distinguish between the Day of the Lord and the Day of Christ are doomed to doctrinal error and private interpretation.

Israel on earth and the Church in Heaven, it is impossible to understand how the events transpire.

Before *"that day"* (the Day of Christ) commences with the Rapture, there is one event specifically mentioned that precedes it. The Bible says there must FIRST be a falling away, an apostasy of believers.[2] A proper understanding of the conditions found in the early Church assists the reader in comprehending this precondition to the commencement of the Day of Christ.

> ***2 Thessalonians 2:3*** *Let no man deceive you by any means (even a letter supposedly from the Paul): for that day (the Day of Christ) shall not come, except there come a **falling away first**, and that man of sin be revealed, the son of perdition;*

Most Bible historians teach that the two Thessalonian epistles were some of Paul's earliest to be written. At the time of Paul's writing to the Thessalonians (AD 51-52), Christianity was young and zealous. The apostle Paul had only been converted about fifteen years prior to penning these letters. According to the postscripts at the end of the epistles, Paul wrote the epistles from Athens—the place he visited shortly after leaving Thessalonica *(Acts 17:1-15)*. At best, these saints had only been exposed to the truths found in Paul's epistles for a few years. These babes in Christ were gaining doctrinal understanding at a rapid pace, but what they lacked in knowledge they possessed in zeal.

Nothing could offer more assurance to these believers than to know that the Day of Christ which commences at the Rapture could not begin apart from a spiritual *"falling away."* Why? These saints witnessed a Heaven-sent spiritual awakening unlike any other throughout man's history. Paul's reference was likely to a falling away that would begin after the apostles died but one being experienced today on a grand scale.

---

[2] Some teachers mock the fact that the Church will be raptured in a state of apostasy rather than at some spiritually evolved and heightened level of achievement. They surmise that the Church should be purged and purified rather than rewarded through a Pre-tribulation Rapture. However, God's salvation of a soul shows God going completely contrary to this philosophy. He died for the ungodly *(Romans 5:6)* and reconciled us while yet His enemies *(Romans 5:10)*. Must the Church of the Last Days earn and deserve God's faithfulness and promised removal as some teach?

This falling away is not a rejection of God by the world, but a defection from the faith by believers. The world cannot fall away from something it never possessed or professed. [3]

During the first century, thousands of converts were coming to Christ (at times during a single gathering—see *Acts 2:41; Acts 4:4*). These believers uniquely understood that the apostasy was yet future. In fact, the culmination of the spiritual apostasy would not take place for almost two millennia. In order for a mass *"falling away"* to occur, believers would need to be convinced concerning the very lies Paul was trying to prevent the Thessalonian believers from accepting. With the moving away from the Pre-tribulation Rapture teaching to Pre-wrath, Post-tribulation positions, Christians are being taught NOT to look for the imminent return of Christ. In fact, they are being taught just the opposite—look for signs—or worse, the Antichrist! As has been previously proven from scripture, Christians without hope are prone to apostasy. First John describes how Christians react when they trust in the Blessed Hope of Christ's return and the Church's departure.

> *1 John 3:3 And **every man that hath this hope in him purifieth himself,** even as he is pure.*

It is imperative to note that the ONLY stipulation preventing the clock from starting on the Day of Christ is this falling away. The Bible does not say, as some mistakenly teach, that the Man of Sin must be re-

---

[3] This falling away did not take place on the grand scale mentioned during Paul's, Peter's, or John's lifetimes, but could easily have been hastened following their deaths. Paul wrote during the first century that spiritual deception was ramping up, *"For we are **not as many, which corrupt the word of God:** but as of sincerity, but as of God, in the sight of God speak we in Christ" (**2 Corinthians 2:17**).* For this reason, among others, it is dangerous to bolster one's faith based upon something considered antiquated. This would include those trusting in something with great antiquity like the writings of those who followed the apostles (i.e., the church fathers). Paul mentioned that there were many who were corrupting God's word even prior to the completion of the inspired canon. One should not attempt to strengthen his faith concerning the veracity of any teaching based upon the antiquity of the writing outside the inspired text. In fact, two primary factors historically enabled documents to gain a prolonged existence: (1) disuse because the Church rejected the writings, and (2) acceptance and preservation by those who notoriously burned both orthodox writers and their writings. The "Dark Ages" lasted 1,000 years (AD 500 to 1500) partly because the haters of God's truths were in control of religion, philosophy, morals, politics, art, and education. God's true believers lived in hiding lest they lose their lives.

vealed FIRST. *2 Thessalonians 2:3* simply continues chronologically and incorporates a gap of time at the comma following the word *first*.[4] This is similar to the gap of time found a few verses later at the comma in verse 8 after the word *revealed*. Neither verse 3 nor verse 8 reveals events that happen simultaneously.

The *"falling away"* equates to the prophecy of the last days' *"perilous times"* (*2 Timothy 3:1*) as evil men will *"wax worse and worse"* (*2 Timothy 3:13*). It is a defection from the faith similar to those who in time of temptation *"fall away"* (*Luke 8:13*), lacking the appropriate foundation. Paul also wrote to Timothy of this *"latter times"* apostasy calling it a *"depart*[ing] *from the faith."* [5]

> *1 Timothy 4:1 Now the Spirit speaketh expressly, that **in the latter times** some shall **depart from the faith**, giving heed to seducing spirits, and doctrines of devils;*

This departure from *"sound doctrine"* (*2 Timothy 4:3*) is a distinguishing feature of the Church's last days. This differs considerably from

---

[4] God provides further proof of how to correctly interpret the grammatical pattern found in *2 Thessalonians 2:3*. The grammatical pattern of "and" followed by a comma reveals a chronological event that does not necessarily take place simultaneously. Here are two additional examples of ", and" that reveals the same scenario and grammatical pattern.

*Revelation 17:8 The beast that thou sawest was, and is not; and shall ascend out of the bottomless pit, **and go into perdition:** and they that dwell on the earth shall wonder, whose names were not written in the book of life from the foundation of the world, when they behold the beast that was, and is not, and yet is.*

*Revelation 17:11 And the beast that was, and is not, even he is the eighth, and is of the seven, **and goeth into perdition.***

The beast which ascends from the bottomless pit in *Revelation 11:7* does not immediately descend into perdition. There is a gap of time in Revelation chapter 17 similar to the one found in *2 Thessalonians 2:3: Let no man deceive you by any means: for that day shall not come, except there come a falling away first, **and** that man of sin be revealed, the son of perdition.* Some claim that the average person would not read or understand the passage "that way!" What really matters is how God intended for the passage to be understood when combined with the full *counsel of God (Acts 20:27)*, not whether a superficial reading allows for any private interpretation *(2 Peter 1:20)* or the correct rendition.

[5] See appendices 3 and 4 for a study on the differences between falling away and departing, especially as it relates to the Greek word *apostasia (ἀποστασία)* and the pre-King James Bible editions.

the last days for the Jews which are marked by physical disturbances (famines, pestilences, earthquakes, etc.) *(Matthew 24:7)*. The Church's last days are highlighted with spiritual disturbances (covetous, boasters, proud, blasphemers, unthankful, etc.) *(2 Timothy 3:1-5)*.[6] Those (whether Pre-tribulation or Post-tribulation teachers) focusing upon the physical signs merely serve as an unfortunate distraction from the true indica-

> The Church's last days are highlighted with spiritual disturbances (covetous, boasters, proud, blasphemers, unthankful, etc.) *(2 Timothy 3:1-5).*

tors of the immediacy of Christ's return. The Church should focus upon the spiritual decay of New Testament Christianity as the only indicator of the last days.

The Man of Sin (2 Thessalonians 2:3-4)

> *2 Thessalonians 2:3 Let no man deceive you by any means (even a letter supposedly from the Paul): for that day (the Day of Christ) shall not come, except there come a falling away first, and that **man of sin be revealed**, the **son of perdition**; 4 Who opposeth and exalteth himself above all that is called God, or that is worshipped; so that he as God sitteth in the temple of God, shewing **himself** that he is God.*

The Bible clearly points out the fact that the spiritual falling away precedes the Day of Christ. Just as clearly, the scripture sets forth that the inception of the Day of Christ precedes the revelation of the Man of Sin. Though not directly stated in Thessalonians, the peacemaker's **entrance** precedes his **revelation** by three and one-half years.

The Man of Sin, who is the Son of Perdition, opposes all that is worshipped and, as such, exalts himself above God. Jesus Himself identified a *son of perdition (John 17:12)* as one whom Satan entered into *(Luke 22:3)*. Prior to the Man of Sin's revelation, he will appear to be a man of peace and will *"obtain the kingdom by flatteries" (Daniel 11:21)*.

Revealed in His Time (2 Thessalonians 2:5-6)

Though the Lord dwells outside of time *(Isaiah 57:15)*, He assigns to everything its time and season upon the earth *(Ecclesiastes 3:1)*. Just

---

[6] See appendix #4 for a comparison between the Church's Last Days and the Last Days of Daniel's Seventieth Week.

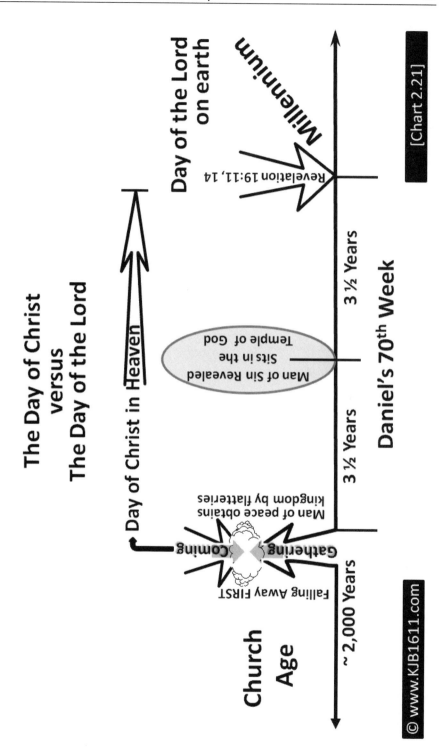

The Day of Christ
versus
The Day of the Lord

Day of the Lord
on earth

Millennium

Revelation 19:11, 14

[Chart 2.21]

Day of Christ in Heaven

Man of Sin Revealed
Sits in the
Temple of God

3 ½ Years

Daniel's 70th Week

3 ½ Years

Man of peace obtains
kingdom by flatteries

Gathering ⟩⟨ Coming

Falling Away FIRST

~ 2,000 Years

Church
Age

© www.KJB1611.com

as the Lord Jesus Christ came *"when the fulness of time was come" (Galatians 4:4)*, and there will come a time when *"the fulness of the Gentiles"* will *"come in" (Romans 11:25, 12)*, the *"man of sin"* will *"be revealed" (2 Thessalonians 2:3) "in his time" (2 Thessalonians 2:6)*.

> *2 Thessalonians 2:5 Remember ye not, that, when I was yet with you, I told you these things? 6 And **now ye know what withholdeth** that he might be revealed **in his time**.*

In this passage, Paul admonished the Thessalonians to reflect **not** upon his first epistle, but upon personal discussions that took place while he was with them. This being said, we should not try to force the context of the current discussion back into first Thessalonians. Those dear saints initially receiving this epistle would know better. By recalling Paul's conversations, they would know WHAT would withhold the Man of Sin's revelation. Knowing Paul's background would lead any reader today to recognize that Paul would have used the Old Testament canon to reveal the WHAT and who.

Some person, event, or thing *withholdeth* the revelation of the Man of Sin. Perhaps the most common teaching among those who subscribe to the Pre-tribulational Rapture is that the *"what"* withholding is the removal of the Spirit of God from the earth.[7] The Spirit of Christ *(Romans 8:9)* indwells Church Age believers and will be removed from that capacity at the Rapture. And while this fact holds true, this teaching comes with its own share of challenges: (1) the removal of that which is withholding occurs **in the middle** of Daniel's Seventieth Week which then allows the revelation of the Man of Sin, (2) the assumption that the Spirit of Christ will not indwell tribulation saints, and (3) zero scriptural evidence of the Spirit of God withholding or holding against the fulfillment of prophecy.

Prior to ascertaining the meaning and context of the passage, one must gain a better understanding of the word *withholdeth*. Historically, the word meant to keep back or refuse to allow. The same appears to be true in scripture *(Genesis 20:6; Genesis 22:12; Job 12:15)*. Apart from the *-eth* ending, the compound word is made up of the prefix *with*

---

[7] See appendix #3 for one of the most common positions amongst Pre-tribulation teachers concerning "the restrainer" being the Church because of the immediate spiritual impact upon the world when all Spirit-indwelled believers suddenly disappear.

meaning "back or away" and the root word *hold* which is self-explanatory.

According to a literal understanding of the passage, some being or thing is going to keep or hold back the revelation of the Man of Sin on this earth until an appointed time midway through Daniel's Seventieth Week. Both the books of Daniel and Revelation indicate that Michael the archangel dutifully *withholds* when warring against the Devil.

> **Both the books of Daniel and Revelation indicate that Michael the archangel dutifully *withholds* when warring against the Devil.**

*Daniel 10:21 But I will shew thee that which is noted in the scripture of truth: and there is none that **holdeth** with me in these things, but **Michael your prince**.*

*Revelation 12:7 And there was war in heaven: **Michael** and his angels **fought against the dragon**; and the dragon fought and his angels, 8 And prevailed not; neither was their place found any more in heaven. 9 And **the great dragon was cast out**, that old serpent, called the Devil, and Satan, which deceiveth the whole world: he was cast out **into the earth**, and his angels were cast out with him.*

The prophecy is clear and unambiguous. Halfway through Daniel's Seventieth Week, Michael wars against the Devil and the Devil is cast down to the earth. At that point, the Bible warns, *"Woe to the inhabiters of the earth" (Revelation 12:12)*. The Devil on earth will no longer be withheld or restrained and all hell will break loose upon the earth, particularly as it relates to Israel.

He Who Now Letteth Will Let (2 Thessalonians 2:7-9)

*2 Thessalonians 2:7 For the **mystery of iniquity** doth already work: only he who now letteth **will let, until he be taken out of the way**. 8 And then shall **that Wicked** be revealed, whom the Lord shall consume with the spirit of his mouth, and shall destroy with the brightness of his coming: 9 Even him, whose coming is after the working of Satan with all power and **signs and lying wonders**,*

The mystery of iniquity is already at work. According to John, *"even now are there many antichrists" (1 John 2:18)*. However, this is not the same manner in which THE Antichrist will work in Daniel's Seventieth Week. When the Week ensues, the Man of Sin will launch his campaign with a platform of peace. By the end of the prophetic week, the Man of Sin's ability to convince the masses will be so that people will boldly proclaim, *"Peace and safety" (1 Thessalonians 5:3).*

One might wonder how Satan could undertake such a massive operation without being exposed for his true identity and motive. However, the Bible indicates that Satan will deceive the masses with *signs and lying wonders (2 Thessalonians 2:9)* elsewhere called *great wonders (Revelation 13:13).* Just as the apostles went forth with signs to confirm their words, the beast will have power to perform signs in hopes of confirming Satan's message.

> *Revelation 13:13 And **he doeth great wonders,** so that he maketh fire come down from heaven on the earth in the sight of men, 14 **And deceiveth** them that dwell on the earth...*

Before one can fully grasp the Man of Sin's revelation, a better understanding of the word *"let"* must be ascertained. The immediate context of *2 Thessalonians 2:7* suggests a meaning somewhat contrary to common usage. Contextually, whatever or whoever letteth does so until taken out of the way. As such, it would appear the word *"let"* is equal to being in the way or withholding *(2 Thessalonians 2:6).* Offering another witness, Paul told those in Rome he had purposed to come unto them, but was *"let"* hitherto *(Romans 1:13)* only to later clarify that he had been much *"hindered"* from coming *(Romans 15:22).*

> *Romans 1:13 Now I would not have you ignorant, brethren, that oftentimes I purposed to come unto you, **(but was let hitherto,)** that I might have some fruit among you also, even as among other Gentiles.*

> *Romans 15:22 For which cause also I have been much **hindered** from coming to you.*[8]

---

[8] Bible reading and Bible study are the Christian's companion bookends for Bible theology and Bible understanding. Therefore, when the reader stumbles across an older word (like "let") or one no longer commonly used in *2 Thessalonians 2:7,* he understands the meaning by comparing scripture with scripture. The Bible use of this word means that something would *hinder* the revelation of the Wicked one. In Romans, Paul was let hitherto (hindered) and someone will let (or hinder) the revelation of the Wicked. The mystery of iniquity is being hindered from its full revelation by the fact that something needs to be taken out of the way first. Who?

Who Is "Taken Out of the Way"?

Most Bible teachers would agree that the Man of Sin is not revealed until the midpoint of Daniel's Seventieth Week. What is not, however, as commonly agreed upon is the identity of the one *"taken out of the way."* By comparing scripture with scripture, it appears that the identity of the one letting or withholding is Michael the archangel, and not as commonly taught, the Church (or indwelled believers who depart this earth 3½ years prior to the Man of Sin's revelation).

> *2 Thessalonians 2:7 For the mystery of iniquity doth already work: only he who now letteth will let, until he be taken out of the way. 8 And **then shall that Wicked be revealed,***

> *Revelation 12:7 And there was **war in heaven**: Michael and his angels fought against the dragon; and the dragon fought and his angels, 8 And prevailed not; neither was their place found any more in heaven. 9 And **the great dragon was cast out**, that old serpent, called the Devil, and **Satan**, which deceiveth the whole world: he **was cast out into the earth**, and his angels were cast out with him.*

Michael, as Israel's prince, is Israel's protector. However, midway through the prophetic Week, Michael will be taken out of the way allowing Satan to work unrestrained on the earth.

> *Daniel 10:13 But the prince of the kingdom of Persia withstood me one and twenty days: but, lo, **Michael, one of the chief princes**, came to help me; and I remained there with the kings of Persia.*

With the Devil's scope pinpointed upon earth's inhabitants and his time short, he will demonstrate great wrath against those upon the earth. Up until this time, Satan's focus day and night entailed standing before God's throne accusing the brethren *(Revelation 12:10)*. While he focused upon this objective, Israel remained safe. When the war in Heaven ensues and Satan is cast into the earth, the real **unbridled trouble begins**. At this time, the Abomination of Desolation takes place, the beast appears, and the Jews must and do flee for safety.

> *Revelation 12:12 Therefore rejoice, ye heavens, and ye that dwell in them. **Woe to the inhabiters of the earth** and of the sea! for the **devil***

Remember that those indwelled by the Comforter whose purpose is to reprove the world of sin *(John 16:13)* left earth 3½ years earlier.

*is come down unto you, having **great wrath**, because he knoweth that he hath but a **short time**.*

***Daniel 12:1** And at that time shall **Michael** stand up, **the great prince which standeth for the children of thy people**: and there shall be a **time of trouble**, such as never was since there was a nation even to that same time: and at that time **thy people shall be delivered**, every one that shall be found written in the book.*

Revelation 13:4** And they worshipped the dragon which gave power unto the beast: and they worshipped the beast, saying, **Who is like unto the beast? who is able to make war with him?

Jeremiah also pinpoints this time and identifies the *it* as **Jacob's Trouble**: *"Alas! for that day is great, so that none is like it: it is even **the time of Jacob's trouble**; but he [Israel] **shall be saved out of it**" (Jeremiah 30:7).* Jeremiah says Jacob (Israel) will be saved out of this time while ***Daniel 12:1*** testifies *"thy people shall be **delivered**."* This truth can be confirmed by comparing those *"saved"* in ***Acts 2:21*** with those *"delivered"* in ***Joel 2:32***. This time of trouble will start at the Abomination of Desolation *(**Matthew 24:15**)* when many will *"flee into the mountains"* for deliverance and protection (verse 16) from the *"great tribulation"* (verse 21).

Understanding the Chronology

Understanding the chronology of the events in Second Thessalonians chapter 2 is imperative. The chapter is laid out chronologically, but not necessarily uninterrupted. The passage begins just prior to Daniel's Seventieth Week and spans the entire seven-year period. Below is the basic overview of the chronology. Take note of two key transitional verses (verses 3 and 8) each spanning 3½ years.

- Verse 3—Falling away first **(precedes 70th Week)** *to* Man of Sin revealed **(Midpoint)**
- Verse 4—Man of Sin sits in temple of God **(Midpoint of Daniel's 70th Week)**
- Verse 6—Revealed in his time **(Midpoint of Daniel's 70th Week)**
- Verse 7—Withholder taken out of the way **(Midpoint of Daniel's 70th Week)**
- Verse 8—Wicked revealed **(Midpoint of Daniel's 70th Week)** *to* destroy with brightness of Christ's coming **(End of Daniel's 70th Week)**

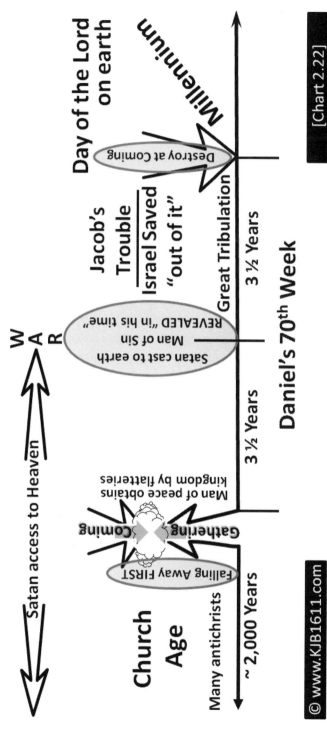

The Revelation of the Man of Sin

Day of the Lord on earth

Millennium

Satan access to Heaven

WAR

Destroy at Coming

Jacob's Trouble

Israel Saved "out of it"

Satan cast to earth
Man of Sin
REVEALED "in his time"

Great Tribulation

Man of peace obtains kingdom by flatteries

Gathering — Coming

Falling Away FIRST

Church Age

Many antichrists

~ 2,000 Years

3 ½ Years

3 ½ Years

Daniel's 70th Week

It's All About the Timing

Every Bible student understands the importance of context. The context of the first half of Second Thessalonians deals with the REVELATION of the Man of Sin/Son of Perdition/Mystery of Iniquity/that Wicked. Just like the book of Revelation is the revelation of Jesus Christ, this passage in Thessalonians is the revelation of Satan. Paul uses the same word to make his point on three separate occasions.

- Verse 3 mentions that *"the man of sin, the son of perdition will be* **revealed**"
- Verse 6 mentions that *"he might be* **revealed** *in HIS TIME"*
- Verse 8: *"and then shall that Wicked be* **revealed**"

The timing of this revelation unveils the Pre-wrath/Post-tribulation dilemma. Each mention of the revelation must be considered in unison in order to understand the timing. The problem with stating that the Man of Sin will be revealed prior the Church's Rapture misses the gap after the FIRST event of verse 3. Verse 8 provides a similar gap, where that Wicked will be revealed, whom the Lord will consume at His coming 3½ years after this revelation takes place. The comma in this phrase spans this 3½ year period. These facts are missed by those blinded by preconceived notions and agendas and those simply fixated upon parroting what they have been taught.

The Not-so-Secret Rapture

The Lord's Revealing: Christ is NOT revealed to the world at the Rapture of the Church. His return for the Church starts in Heaven *(1 Thessalonians 4:17)* but stops with the gathering in the clouds *(1 Thessalonians 4:18)*. Because He is not revealed to the world at the Rapture, some Pre-tribulation teachers coined the awkward phrase, the *"secret Rapture."* Obviously, the world will be acutely aware that the Rapture has taken place when so many disappear from the earth *(1 Thessalonians 4:17)*. The world may even hear the *shout* from the voice of the archangel or the *trump of God (1 Thessalonians 4:16)*. Yet, the Lord does not reveal Himself to earth's inhabitants at that time. Those left upon the earth will not attribute any part of this phenomenon to God's blessings upon the Church, nor will they repent after having missed the Rapture, nor will they glorify God.

For this reason, it is important to note the exact timing that the revelation of Jesus Christ takes place. His revelation happens on the Day of the Lord at the end of Daniel's Seventieth Week. The book of Luke uses the example of Lot to point out that the Lord will be *revealed* at the Second Advent (when He takes out His vengeance upon an unrepentant world).

> *Luke 17:29 But the same day that Lot went out of Sodom it rained fire and brimstone from heaven, and destroyed them all. 30 Even thus shall it be in the day **when the Son of man is revealed.***

Though frequently misapplied, Lot is NOT a picture of the Church's Rapture. He represents those who are supernaturally gathered, not the gathering of *2 Thessalonians 2:1,* but the gathering together upon earth *(Matthew 24:31)* after being warned to flee without so much as looking back *(Luke 17:31-32)*. As soon as the earthly saints are gathered, the Saviour will be revealed and His vengeance unleashed.[9]

> *2 Thessalonians 1:7 And to you who are troubled rest with us, when the Lord Jesus shall be **revealed from heaven** with his mighty angels, 8 In flaming fire **taking vengeance** on them that know not God, and that obey not the gospel of our Lord Jesus Christ:*

In this passage, Paul confirms the timing of the Lord's revelation. Notice that the Lord's revelation takes place when He returns *from Heaven (Revelation 19:11)*. Some Post-tribulationists teach that the Rapture found in Thessalonians takes place as believers are caught up to meet the Lord in the clouds only to immediately return to earth. Many scriptures contradict this horizontal coming back to earth by stating that the Lord will be revealed and return to earth after Heaven opens *(Revelation 19:11)*.

A Strong Delusion (2 Thessalonians 2:10-12)

> *2 Thessalonians 2:10 And with all deceivableness of unrighteousness in them that perish; because they received not the love of the truth, that they might be saved. 11 And for this cause **God shall send them strong delusion, that they should believe a lie:** 12 That they all might be damned who believed not the truth, but had pleasure in unrighteousness.*

---

[9] The first five words of the last book of the Bible are *"The Revelation of Jesus Christ."* This book expressly contains the details of His revelation to the world on the Day of the Lord when *"the kingdoms of this world are become the kingdoms of our Lord" (Revelation 11:15)*. See also *Obadiah 15 and 21.*

When the Man of Sin enters earth's scene, he will do so as a man of peace. As he ushers in peace throughout the Middle East, he will have accomplished the unimaginable. He will be viewed as a saviour by the world's inhabitants. Though this peace will be fleeting, it will deceive vast multitudes including a great number of Jews.[10] One would think that the Abomination of Desolation would be enough to open mankind's eyes causing a general rebellion against such wickedness. The Bible reveals otherwise.

Those who *"received not the love the truth, that they might be saved" (2 Thessalonians 2:10)* and *"believed not the truth, but had pleasure in unrighteousness" (2 Thessalonians 2:12)* will be sent a *"strong delusion, that they should believe a lie" (2 Thessalonians 2:11)*. This is an altogether different situation from man choosing wilful ignorance. This blindness will not come from within the individual but from above; it is a God-sent delusion!

Regardless of whether someone has rejected the gospel prior to the Church's departure or will do so during the first 3½ years of Daniel's Seventieth Week, the truth remains apparent. These people chose not to believe the truth when it required faith without sight; therefore, God prohibits them from seeing the truth when the lie becomes so apparent that its rejection requires little-to-no faith. For this reason, only a fool rejects the current light in favour of waiting until Daniel's Seventieth Week.

Hope of any spiritual illumination is quite scarce in the Tribulation. After the multitudes are killed *(Revelation 7:9)*, only a remnant of Jews and some enlightened nations will be left to reject the power and rule of the Devil and his unholy trinity. The rest of mankind, those who have and will reject the truth of God's word, will be damned; not because God wills or wants these people to receive damnation *(2 Peter 3:9)*, but because His justice demands repentance and they repeatedly refused to repent when given several opportunities *(Revelation 9:20-21, Revelation 16:9-11)*.

---

[10] Even today, should a political leader arrive on the scene who could offer such peace, the masses would unwisely give up their rights and liberties for such an outcome. Welcome to the globalist agenda.

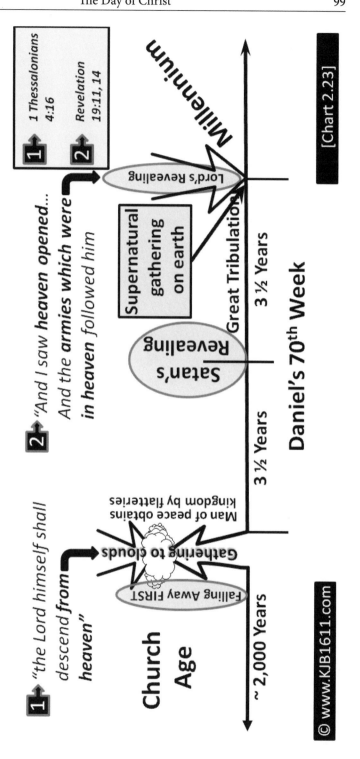

The Lord's Heavenly Descending

1 "the Lord himself shall descend from heaven"

2 "And I saw heaven opened... And the armies which were in heaven followed him"

| 1 | 1 Thessalonians 4:16 |
| 2 | Revelation 19:11, 14 |

Millennium

Lord's Revealing

Satan's Revealing

Supernatural gathering on earth

Gathering to clouds

Man of peace obtains kingdom by flatteries

Falling Away FIRST

Church Age

~ 2,000 Years

3 ½ Years

Great Tribulation

Daniel's 70th Week

3 ½ Years

[Chart 2.23]

Chosen to Salvation (2 Thessalonians 2:13-14)

Context solves the vast majority of scriptural perplexities and protects Bible students from dangerous assumptions. Ignoring any passage's context frequently generates interpretations that are irresponsible, detrimental, and sometimes damnable to its adherents. However, private interpretation of scripture is quite common amongst far too many Bible teachers. The following passage serves as a case in point.

> *2 Thessalonians 2:13 But we are bound to give thanks alway to God for you, brethren beloved of the Lord, because **God hath from the beginning chosen you to salvation** through sanctification of the Spirit and belief of the truth: 14 Whereunto **he called you** by our gospel, **to the obtaining of the glory of our Lord Jesus Christ**.*

The subject passage above has led many people to believe that God, from the beginning, which they define as the creation of the world, chose only a certain segment of humanity to be born again (spiritually saved). Nothing could be further from the truth. Within the passage's context, the astute Bible student sees that it teaches nothing of the sort. In fact, the context identifies the salvation to which these saints were chosen *(2 Thessalonians 2:13)* as *"the obtaining of the glory of our Lord Jesus Christ" (2 Thessalonians 2:14)*. This *"obtaining of the glory"* of Christ takes place at the Rapture of the Church (also known as the Adoption).

> *Romans 8:23 And not only they, but ourselves also, which have the firstfruits of the Spirit, even we ourselves groan within ourselves, **waiting for the adoption**, to wit, **the redemption of our body**.*

The context of the passage actually serves as a reminder that the saints of God will be *saved* from Daniel's Seventieth Week through physical deliverance not afforded to those who have rejected Christ. This salvation includes a deliverance from the deceptive, peaceful entry of the Man of Sin, the revelation of the same, the Abomination of Desolation, the strong delusion, and the entirety of Daniel's Seventieth Week, etc.

This usage of the word *salvation* (meaning a physical deliverance) is prominent throughout the greatest portion of scripture. In fact, the apostle Paul frequently incorporated the term (salvation) in various forms to describe physical deliverance *(Romans 5:9; Philippians 1:19; 1 Timothy 2:15)* rather than limiting it to a soteriological application of the soul's salvation *(Romans 1:16, Romans 10:13; 1 Corinthians 1:18, 21; Ephe-*

The Adoption & Redemption of the Body

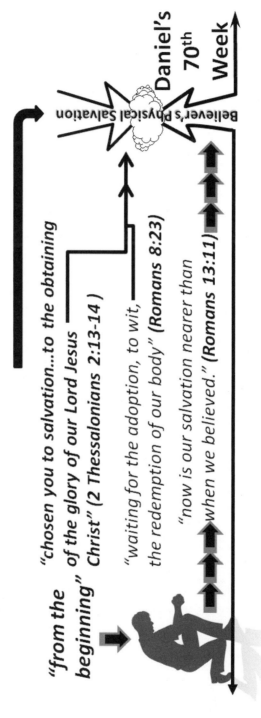

"from the beginning"

"chosen you to salvation...to the obtaining of the glory of our Lord Jesus Christ" (2 Thessalonians 2:13-14)

"waiting for the adoption, to wit, the redemption of our body" (Romans 8:23)

"now is our salvation nearer than when we believed." (Romans 13:11)

Believer's Physical Salvation

Daniel's 70th Week

Church Age

[Chart 2.24]

sians 1:13, Ephesians 2:5, 8). Those who read the soul's salvation into every usage of *saved* or *salvation* are guaranteed one outcome— deviating from sound theology and even digressing into heretical teachings.

While this fact is true, an even more convincing argument in the Thessalonian epistles reveals that Paul only used **saved** *(1 Thessalonians 2:16; 2 Thessalonians 2:10)* and **salvation** in reference to a physical salvation *(1 Thessalonians 5:8, 9; 2 Thessalonians 2:13)*. Again, the five usages of these two terms (saved or salvation) in the Thessalonian epistles were never in reference to the salvation of the soul from Hell.

Some Bible teachers have further compounded the error by assuming that the word *beginning* found in **2 Thessalonians 2:13** infers an event from the foundation of the world. However, the passage gives absolutely no reason to make any such assumption. On the contrary, as it pertains to the Thessalonians, the beginning was a time associated to their belief of the truth and sanctification by the Spirit. In other words, this beginning pointed to the time when they became new-born babes in Christ. It was at this new birth that God chose them to be delivered from any wrath to come including that which occurs during Daniel's Seventieth Week *(1 Thessalonians 5:9)*.

> At the Rapture of the Church, our salvation will be complete.

It is imperative to note that our salvation is both a spiritual and physical deliverance. We have been spiritually saved and anticipate our physical salvation which is *"nearer than when we believed" (Romans 13:11)*. As the old maxim goes, "every Christian is presently two-thirds saved." Our *soul* is redeemed, our *spirit* has been quickened, but we still deal with our *body* of flesh as it awaits its redemption. At the Rapture of the Church, our salvation will be complete—our body will be redeemed *(Romans 8:23)* or changed *(1 Corinthians 15:51-58)* that it may be fashioned like unto Christ's glorious body *(Philippians 3:21)*.

It is at this point in salvation that we will truly obtain *"the glory of our Lord Jesus Christ" (2 Thessalonians 2:14)*. Another important and imperative point not to miss: the context of the passage plainly does *not* teach some Calvinistic concept where some in the beginning of time are chosen for Heaven and some chosen for Hell! That is wicked, heretical, and contrary to the nature of God who is not willing than any should perish.

*2 Peter 3:9 **The Lord is** not slack concerning his promise, as some men count slackness; but is longsuffering to us-ward, **not willing that any should perish, but that all should come to repentance.***

Stand Fast, Comfort Your Hearts, and Work (2 Thessalonians 2:15-17)

*2 **Thessalonians 2:15** Therefore, brethren, **stand fast**, and hold the traditions which ye have been taught, whether by word, or our epistle. 16 Now our Lord Jesus Christ himself, and God, even our Father, which hath loved us, and hath given us everlasting consolation and good hope through grace, 17 **Comfort your hearts**, and stablish you in every good word **and work**.*

It is evident from reading these epistles that these saints had been through a fiery test concerning their *"good hope through grace."* They had faced both a direct and an indirect assault upon their faith concerning the Lord Jesus Christ's coming for the Church. Their fervent zeal for the work of God had been replaced by a fear of coming Tribulation. After yet another reminder of the physical salvation to come, the apostle

> Saints who lose sight of the impending return of Christ lose their desire for two things: (1) an inward purity and (2) a zealous, godly service.

concluded by encouraging these saints in three basic areas: (1) stand fast in what you have been taught, (2) comfort your hearts, and (3) get busy working for the Lord. Failure in any one of these three admonitions was bound to create discomfort, discouragement, and disunity. The same holds true today.

These saints had been taught that the Church was destined for glory rather than punishment. Unfortunately, they had lost this hope in God's unwavering promises. However, the apostle Paul charged them to *"stand fast"* in or *"hold"* those traditions they had been taught both in person by Paul and through the epistles. As he stated in First Thessalonians chapter 4, they needed to use this hope as a means of heartfelt *comfort*, both personally and toward others. Perhaps of even greater assurance was that their hope's return would bring with it a renewed desire to serve the Lord. Saints who lose sight of the impending return of Christ lose their desire for two things: (1) an inward purity and (2) a zealous, godly service. It was time for these saints to rekindle both aspects destroyed by those who sought to confuse.

The Bible nowhere indicates that God intends for Daniel's Seventieth Week to serve as punishment or purification of the Church, nor did He have any group other than Israel in mind for all 490 years of Daniel's Seventy Weeks

10

The Lord Direct Your Hearts

Second Thessalonians Chapter 3

2 Thessalonians 3:4-5

Before closing what would be the last inspired epistle to these dear saints, Paul set forth two final admonitions. These believer's faith had been attacked, their hope devastated; however, the Lord would repair that which was broken. First, he encouraged them to allow their hearts to be directed of the Lord to patiently wait for Christ. As is always the case, God's love would be the balm of healing. The outcome would be a restored looking and longing for Jesus.

> These believer's faith had been attacked, their hope devastated; however, the Lord would repair that which was broken. First,[Paul] encouraged them to allow their hearts to be directed of the Lord to patiently wait for Christ.

> *2 Thessalonians 3:4 And we have confidence in the Lord touching you, that ye both do and will do the things which we command you.*
> *5 And **the Lord direct your hearts** into the love of God, and **into the patient waiting for Christ**.*

Secondly, Paul used some of his sternest speech toward these dear saints. He **commanded** them to cut off fellowship with those who had robbed them of their hope.

> *2 Thessalonians 3:6 Now **we command** you, brethren, in the name of our Lord Jesus Christ, **that ye withdraw yourselves from every***

brother that walketh disorderly, and not after the tradition which he received of us.

Paul's reference to "tradition" was not man-made traditions like those rebuked by the Lord *(Mark 7:8, 9, 13, etc.)* but denoted the godly instructions given to them. Failure to end these harmful relationships would only repeat the vicious cycle that had cost these saints both their joy and potentially their reward. It can be certain that those who had spread this hopeless message were simply hirelings sent by Satan. Satan's purpose was to rob God's people of all the benefits enjoyed in a life lived in

> It can be certain that those who had spread this hopeless message were simply hirelings sent by Satan. Satan's purpose was to rob God's people of all the benefits enjoyed by a life lived in longing expectation of a soon coming Saviour.

longing expectation of a soon coming Saviour. As such, Paul concludes with the following admonition:

2 Thessalonians 3:14 And if any man obey not our word by this epistle, note that man, and have no company with him, that he may be ashamed.

The apostle warned that there might be some within the body in Thessalonica who had been ill-affected and refused to repent. These people were to be noted and company with them severed. Why? Because they needed to feel the shame associated with refusing to adhere to sound doctrine, especially something as important as the Lord's return for believers. Though fellowship may be severed because of doctrinal differences, Paul concludes by advising that others should be admonished in the spirit of meekness and not looked upon as enemies because of their disagreement.

2 Thessalonians 3:15 Yet count him not as an enemy, but admonish him as a brother.

11

Concluding Thoughts

Second Thessalonians

The Bible consistently fits together without error or ambiguity regardless of the manifold opinions to the contrary. This applies directly to prophecy contained in the scriptures too! Yet, sincere Christians reside on every side of the Rapture timing debate. Despite the opposing viewpoints, Peter specifically states that Bible prophecy is not open to ANY private interpretation.

> **2 Peter 1:20** *Knowing this first, that* ***no prophecy of the scripture is of any private interpretation.***

Man must simply allow the Bible to say what God intended for it to say, nothing more and nothing less. When Bible teachers and students eliminate private interpretation, the truth becomes quite clear. Unfortunately, far too many people enter Bible study with preconceived notions based upon something other than God's perfect word. In fact, far too many people involved in the dialog bring with them their own hidden agendas. Prophecy teachings must be framed by those who consider all the counsel of God while also considering any perceived contradiction within their particular position. Yet, the debate rages.

> [S]incere Christians reside on every side of the Rapture timing debate. Despite the opposing viewpoints, Peter specifically states that Bible prophecy is not open to ANY private interpretation.

False Prophecy: The Root Causes

Throughout history, mankind has been plagued by two root sins (pride and the love of money). Unfortunately, these sins are not limited to those in the world but have also tainted those involved in the gospel ministry. Average churchgoers (along with ex-churchgoers) have grown frustrated by the pride and arrogancy of those "in the ministry." Combine these unsavory traits with the constant appeal for money and you have a recipe for spiritual disillusionment on a grand scale. This is probably why the Lord impressed upon the apostle Paul the necessity of warning Timothy (the pastor at Ephesus) concerning these two stumbling blocks.

> *1 Timothy 3:6 Not a novice, lest being **lifted up with pride** he fall into the condemnation of the devil.*

> *1 Timothy 6:10 For **the love of money is the root of all evil**: which while some coveted after, they have erred from the faith, and pierced themselves through with many sorrows.*

Those motivated by pride and enamoured by money eventually fail to minster to God's people. Their motivations become skewed toward drawing attention toward themselves and drawing disciples toward their particular viewpoint. The damage is immeasurable and the spiritual casualties incalculable.

As Paul passed through Thessalonica, he offered the believers *hope (1 Thessalonians 1:3; 1 Thessalonians 2:19; 1 Thessalonians 4:13; 1 Thessalonians 5:8, etc.)* concerning their future departure at Christ's appearing *(Titus 2:13)*. Hope is both contagious and uncontrollable unless it can be extinguished by an irrepressible fear, especially something founded upon supposed Bible truths. Unfortunately, fear has always been the tool of choice for the *attention-grabbers* and *disciple-drawers* because fear induces misguided actions.[1] These false teachers look for a new angle to gather their followings and unsuspecting disciples.

> [F]ear has always been the tool of choice for the *attention-grabbers* and *disciple-drawers* because fear induces misguided actions.

---

[1] The fear induced is not the *"godly fear" (Hebrews 12:28)* produced by godly sorrow *(2 Corinthians 7:11)*.

History Repeats Itself

Some teachers like Timothy *(1 Thessalonians 3:2)* passed through Thessalonica reinforcing what Paul had already taught the believers. These faithful preachers found receptive ears amongst the spiritually grounded believers. However, there were others in Thessalonica who chose to cast doubt upon the truths taught by Paul. These men garnered the attention they so desperately craved. Ultimately, they turned hearts away from the truth by inciting fear within God's people resulting in uncertainty and confusion. As much as we think things have changed, the most effective first century practices continue to thrive today in our sin-sick world.

Today, some of the most successful insurance agents, financial advisors, lawyers, politicians, and, yes, preachers are those who incite fear within the hearts of others. Regardless of how much we could wish this were not a true assessment, its accuracy remains irrefutable. Despite man's inward propensities, the ministry must NEVER be used as a means to gain attention or seek personal notoriety. Yet, so-called men of God seem always to be looking for a new niche to garner attention, all at the expense of God's unadulterated truths.

> Despite man's inward propensities, the ministry must NEVER be used as a means to gain attention or seek personal notoriety. Yet, so-called men of God seem always to be looking for a new niche to garner attention, all at the expense of God's unadulterated truths.

Their goal: draw away disciples to themselves and away from those who desire to teach the unvarnished truth of God's word. **Their dual motives:** pride and money.

Those perverting the plain teachings of scripture and set on inciting fear ought to consider another type of fear. Instead of encouraging God's people to fear the Tribulation, or the Antichrist, or earthquakes, or famines, or imprisonments, they should consider encouraging God's people to return to a healthy biblical fear of God.[2] Instead of motivating a fear of

---

[2] *1 Peter 2:17 Honour all men. Love the brotherhood. **Fear God.** Honour the king.*

*Ecclesiastes 12:13 Let us hear the conclusion of the whole matter: **Fear God,** and keep his commandments: for this is the whole duty of man.*

losing earthly treasures (homes, food, or health), these preachers should remind people to live in such a way as to not lose their heavenly treasures and rewards.

> *2 Timothy 4:8 Henceforth there is laid up for me **a crown of righteousness**, which the Lord, the righteous judge, **shall give** me at that day: and not to me only, but **unto all them also that love his appearing.***

This *crown of righteousness* will be given to all those who have loved and longed for Christ's appearing. However, those looking for the Tribulation, the Antichrist, or even the two witnesses, or 144,000 are NOT wholeheartedly looking for Christ's appearing. They are looking for signs which Jesus said was indicative of *"a wicked and adulterous generation" (Matthew 16:4).* Those looking for signs contrary to the plain teachings of scripture are walking by sight and not by faith *(2 Corinthians 5:7).*

This lack of spiritual focus results in a loss of hope in the Blessed Hope—that Jesus could come today. The Blessed Hope reminds us that we need to get busy both in our service for the Lord and in our personal purity. Simply put, Christians need to *live* as though Jesus could come today and *prepare* for the inevitable trials and tribulations that face Christians in this sin-sick, Christ-less generation. What are YOU *looking for (Titus 2:13, 2 Peter 3:12)*?

> [T]hose looking for the Tribulation, the Antichrist, or even the two witnesses, or 144,000 are NOT wholeheartedly looking for Christ's appearing. They are looking for signs which Jesus said was indicative of *"a wicked and adulterous generation" (Matthew 16:4).*

Afterword

First & Second Thessalonians

The study of eschatology (or the end-times) allows man to understand the course and direction of humanity along with that of the spirit world. As man approaches the urgency of the hour, earth's inhabitants remain fast asleep or completely distracted by gadgets, gizmos and amusements. In fact, the Church has grown weary in well doing *(2 Thessalonians 3:13, Galatians 6:9)* and has lost any heightened state of expectancy.

With all the confusing and conflicting man-induced prophecies and complacency at epidemic proportions, some of the most pertinent questions remain a mystery for most Christians.

- How prominent should end-time teachings be in the midst of these end-times?
- Does the Church find its complete existence in the approximate 2,000 year interval after Daniel's sixty-ninth Week yet before the commencement of any part of the Seventieth Week *(Daniel 9:24-27)*?
- Is the study of prophecy, as some claim, really just an irrelevant distraction from the more pressing concerns facing the Church and humanity?
- With all the divisiveness and camps, can anyone find assurance in the study of God's word?
- Should the Church be looking for signs *(2 Corinthians 5:7)*? Or does looking for signs indicate a lack of living by faith (signs vs. sight)?
- Should we distinguish between Israel and the Church? Does God have a distinctive prophetic plan for each?
- Does the Lord want man to stake his life and wellbeing upon a certain and ascertainable truth of God's word?

It is never wrong to ask questions of God. In fact, for the Bible student these questions often lead to sound answers from God's holy word. Bible study is much like detective work. In order to find the proper answers

> Bible study is much like detective work. In order to find the proper answers one must be willing to ask the right questions.

one must be willing to ask the right questions. For example, asking the right questions as it pertains to the end-times will show that there are incompatible distinctions between the Rapture of the Church and Christ's Second Advent.

Incompatible Distinctions

The primary passages on the Rapture *(1 Thessalonians 4:13-18, 1 Corinthians 15:51-58, etc.)* are completely distinct from those pertaining to the Second Coming *(Matthew 24:29-31, Zechariah 14:1-21, Revelation 19:11-14, etc.)*. The Second Coming passages alert the Lord's people by carefully and extensively itemizing details of Christ's Second Advent. These same details (and warnings) are absent in the Rapture passages which do not contain any mention of signs. For instance, consider this promise concerning the Lord's Second Advent:

> *Matthew 24:33 So likewise ye, **when ye shall see all these things**, know that it is near, even at the doors.*

Is this admonition directed toward the Church? No! The Second Coming includes an assorted listing of events, yet the Bible always reflects the Rapture as a completely distinct and separate event. Nowhere in scripture does the Second Advent include the Rapture as one of its elements. In fact, critics of the Pre-tribulation Rapture cannot point to a single scripture offering a clear connection and correlation of the Rapture and the Second Advent.

The Bible sets every passage dealing with the Second Coming in the context of worldwide judgment and a period of unprecedented worldwide tribulation. Conversely, the Rapture passages are completely silent concerning any such distress. Additionally, the Second Coming passages are completely silent concerning the Rapture of believers prior to the clearly delineated distress upon earth's inhabitants.

We are told that the Lord gathers the nations against Jerusalem to battle with the inhabitants taken into captivity, and then the Bible says He returns to fight against those nations. These Second Advent passages have no bearing or relationship to the Rapture.

> You may find that your study of the end-times leads to new yet unanswered difficulties concerning the Church and Israel.

*Zechariah 14:3 Then shall **the LORD go forth, and fight against those nations**, as when he fought in the day of battle.*

Questions produce answers; however, not always immediate ones. Sometimes the answers received merely create new questions. You may find that your study of the end-times leads to new yet unanswered difficulties concerning the Church and Israel.

Irreconcilable Quandaries of the Church and Israel in the Tribulation

- Are Jesus' earthly pronouncements more precisely directed toward any particular group, namely Israel? Can the Olivet Discourse apply primarily to Israel and still have application to the Church? If Israel again becomes prominent, how does this reconcile with scriptural admonitions given concerning the elimination of such distinctions within the Body of Christ?
- Will Israel and the Church during Daniel's Seventieth Week be governed by two sets of regulations (the Law and the Gospel)?
- During the Tribulation period, will the 144,000 male Jewish virgins *(Revelation 14:1-5)* be a part of the Church or will the Church become an exclusively Gentile Church completely distinct from the Jewish people during this time?
- Will the Jews preach a completely different *Gospel of the Kingdom (Matthew 4:23, 9:35, 24:14)* from the Gentiles *(Acts 20:24, Galatians 2:2)*?
- Granted, the Millennium will find the Church's existence alongside national Israel but after the Church's departure at the Rapture, membership within the Body of Christ will have been completed, its ranks closed, and its membership glorified.

- If the Church is on earth during the Tribulation, will its members be sealed by the Spirit of God and eternally secure *(Ephesians 1:13, 4:30)*? If so, should Christians concern themselves with a Mark *(Revelation 13:17)* that guarantees the certainty of eternal damnation *(Revelation 19:20)*? In other words, if a Christian cannot lose his salvation, should he be cautioned concerning taking a Mark that would cause the loss of salvation?

The truth is, you may still have questions after reading this book. That is both understandable and expected. What is neither understandable or expected is to question God Himself. As such, write out your questions and seek solutions within God's word. Once the answers are found, trust God! Failure to do so is to willfully sin against God.

> [W]rite out your questions and seek solutions within God's word. Once the answers are found, trust God!

Conclusion

First & Second Thessalonians

It must be understood that there are no irrelevant issues pertaining to biblical interpretation or Bible study. We should endeavour, therefore, to be like the apostle Paul who devoted much time and attention to prophecy. He also claimed to have never shunned declaring *all the counsel of God (Acts 20:27)*. Bible prophecy is part of *the counsel of God.*

> [T]here have been good men, along with unsavory characters (Darby, Irving, etc.), on both sides of the Pre-tribulation Rapture debate.

However, we must insure that our doctrine concerning Bible prophecy originates with the Lord and His word.

Our beliefs are not to be based upon men like Gabelein, Scofield, R.A. Torrey, Harry A. Ironside, Lewis Sperry Chafer, etc. In fact, there have been good men, along with unsavory characters (Darby, Irving, etc.), on both sides of the Pre-tribulation Rapture debate. Our hope rests not in the players or their spirituality but solely upon, *"What saith the scripture."* Our faith does not rest upon what any man or group has taught and people should never become the focus. Paul warned of those in the first century who perverted the scriptures even before the completion of the canon.

> *2 Corinthians 2:17 For we are not as many, which corrupt the word of God: but as of sincerity, but as of God, in the sight of God speak we in Christ.*

Should we accept or reject Bible teachings primarily based upon their association to a person's character or past? No! It is dangerous to elevate guilt-by-association to the pinnacle that some have. Consider some the unsavory accounts and actions by Bible characters greatly used of God:

- Paul was a Christian killer
- Peter was a Christ-denier
- Moses was a murderer
- Lot chose to live amongst the most perverted of earth's inhabitants. After escaping God's judgment, Lot's daughters seduced him yielding incestuous children.
- David murdered an innocent man in order to hide an adulterous relationship with the man's wife.
- Noah got drunk
- Mary Magdalene was a prostitute
- Rahab was a harlot and a pagan Canaanite
- Ruth was a pagan Moabite
- Bathsheba had an adulterous relationship with the man who murdered her husband

Instead of asking what Darby taught, we should be asking *"what saith the Lord."* Instead of looking to fallible man, we should place 100% of our focus upon the infallibility of scripture. One's faith placed upon a teacher because of his present apparent purity can be quite deceptive in the end. Think about it, Lucifer was perfect when he was created *(Ezekiel 28:15)* and yet became the one who would deceive the whole world *(Revelation 12:9)*. Satan loves to associate truth with fallible humans and then use every device within his arsenal to tarnish the truth by blemishing the character of the individual.

> Instead of asking what Darby taught, we should be asking *"what saith the Lord."* Instead of looking to fallible man, we should place 100% of our focus upon the infallibility of scripture.

Many who shun the Pre-tribulation Rapture do so, at least in the beginning, due to some supposed evil associations with those who promoted the teaching in the past. Surely this teaching could not be accurate if those who taught it in the past were corrupt in any way. Once man's holiness becomes the focal point for truth, the Devil then convinces these same men that the Church should be punished for its lack of resolve and worldly contamination. While this is certainly understandable, the members of Christ's Body, the Church, have never in themselves been spotless while still on earth. Yet, Christ paid the penalty for sin individually, collectively and completely through His finished work upon Calvary. Concerning those who emphasize escaping wrath, the wrath of God is already present today, but never upon the Church.

> **Romans 1:18** *For* **the wrath of God is revealed from heaven** *against all ungodliness and unrighteousness of men, who hold the truth in unrighteousness;*

> **Ephesians 5:6** *Let no man deceive you with vain words: for* **because of these things cometh the wrath of God** *upon the children of disobedience.*

> **Colossians 3:6 For which things' sake the wrath of God cometh** *on the children of disobedience:*

Though the wrath of God is present already, there is an undeniable appointment to a future day of wrath and revelation of the righteous judgment of God.

> **Romans 2:5** *But after thy hardness and impenitent heart treasurest up unto thyself wrath* **against the day of wrath and revelation of the righteous judgment of God;**

Just as the church is exempt from God's wrath today, it will not be on the receiving end of God's wrath tomorrow, during Daniel's Seventieth Week, or for any part of eternity. God does not direct His wrath toward the Body of Christ but supernaturally protects us. This is why the argument concerning escaping wrath through the Rapture is a moot point. The wrath exists today and will tomorrow and the Church's Rapture is based upon the Blessed Hope and not simply a Blessed Escape.

> Just as the church is exempt from God's wrath today, it will not be on the receiving end of God's wrath tomorrow, during Daniel's Seventieth Week, or for any part of eternity.

Four Primary Choices for Pre-millennialists:
1) Pre-tribulation Rapture
2) Mid-tribulation Rapture
3) Pre-wrath Rapture
4) Post-tribulation Rapture

Only a Pre-tribulation Rapture eschatology allows for the proper biblical division between Israel and the Church

Pinpointing Daniel's 70 Weeks

Appendix #1

More than at any other time in history, people are questioning the meaning and application of Daniel's Seventy Weeks. These weeks (of years) cover 490 total years and focus primarily upon two distinct events. First, this period specifically relates to God's judgment upon Israel for their lack of faithfulness. Secondly, this period covers God's timetable of events shortly preceding Christ's establishment of His earthly millennial Kingdom.

Much insight comes from exploring two of the most vocal groups questioning the foundational principles of this fundamental eschatology. The first group wonders whether there still remains a future seven-year period as envisioned by Daniel and recorded in Daniel chapter 9. The other equally vocal group believes the Church's destiny includes entering into some or most of this future period of divine judgment upon Israel and the unbelieving world. Both positions are equally disconcerting!

> Recognizing the historical fulfillment as well as the prophetic significance [of Daniel's Seventy Weeks] reveals God's purpose and plan. This period spans over 2,500 years consisting of three distinct time periods of seven weeks, sixty-two weeks, and one week.

Daniel 9:24 expresses the seven comprehensive purposes of Daniel's Seventy Weeks along with setting forth the details of this entire period. Recognizing the historical fulfillment as well as the prophetic significance reveals God's purpose and plan. This period spans over 2,500 years consisting of three distinct time periods of seven weeks, sixty-two weeks, and one week. God further splits the final week of seven years into two halves designated by forty-two months or 1,260 days, or time, times, and half a time (*time* equalling one year).

These three 3½-year designations refer to events that span either the first or last half of the entire seven-year period. It is important to understand the significance for God's emphasis placed upon the dividing of this period into two equal parts. The midpoint of Daniel's Seventieth Week is a defined point of demarcation allowing the astute Bible student to pinpoint the other prophesied events and time periods with precision.

But first . . .

A little background. Studying the genealogies beginning with Adam reveals that the time covered up until Christ's birth consists of 4,004 years. Additionally, the New Testament, which predominantly applies to the Church Age, is not in force until the death of the testator, Jesus Christ *(Hebrews 9:16-17)*.

We also should recognize that the Church Age begins and ends at specifically defined points. It begins shortly following Christ's crucifixion and ends at the Rapture of the Church. The Bible does not indicate any overlapping at the end of the Church Age and God's dealings with Israel. The beginning of the Church Age is followed by God expressly redirecting His focus away from Israel and upon the Gentiles *(Acts 13:44-46; 18:5-6; 28:25-28)*. Those who rightly divide the word of truth according to *2 Timothy 2:15* understand these important truths.

The Church's Blessed Hope

The Rapture known as *The Blessed Hope (Titus 2:13)* has always been a source of encouragement to Christians and serves as the end times' bookend for the Church Age *(1 Thessalonians 1:10; 2:19; 3:13; 4:13-18; 5:8-11, 23, etc.)*. This Blessed Hope refers to the resurrection of those dead "in Christ" and the translation into Heaven of those yet alive when the Lord returns for His body *(1 Corinthians 12:27)*. All Bible-believing prophecy teachers refer to the Rapture as the next great event to take place upon God's prophetic timetable.

Those who incorrectly champion the Mid-tribulation, or Pre-wrath, or Post-tribulation Rapture positions do *not* believe that the next prophetic event will be the Rapture of the Church. In fact, instead of looking for Christ *(Philippians 3:20; Titus 2:13)*, each of these groups believe and teach that Christians should be looking for the signing of the treaty with Israel, or the Abomination of Desolation, or the two Tribulation Witnesses to appear, or one of the Tribulation period earthquakes, or the blood moon that takes place during the sixth seal, or the sun being darkened, or the stars falling from Heaven, or any combination of these yet future prophetic events. This is contrary to scripture!

> Yet, Christians are never told *to* prepare for nor *how to* prepare for Daniel's Seventieth Week or the Antichrist's reign of terror. Surely, the apostle Paul would have been led to offer Church Age saints some form of explicit guidance to withstand this terrible time.

The Bible nowhere tells **Christians** to be looking for any of those events! One thing for sure, these teachers do not believe that we should be looking for Christ to return *first*. Yet, Christians are never told *to* prepare for nor *how to* prepare for Daniel's Seventieth Week or the Antichrist's reign of terror. Surely, the apostle Paul would have been led to offer Church Age saints some form of explicit guidance to withstand this terrible time.

According to scripture, Christians need to be looking for Jesus. That's why the Lord's return for His "body" is called the "Blessed Hope." These truths have offered great *comfort (1 Thessalonians 4:18; 5:11)* and *hope (1 Thessalonians 2:19; Titus 2:13)* to countless generations. The Church should be constantly and consistently working while awaiting His soon coming. Following the Church's departure, scripture immediately directs man's focus away from the Church now absent and reverts focus back upon the nation of Israel.

Daniel's Seventieth Week (Chart #1)

Daniel's Seventieth Week (as defined in Daniel chapter 9) begins by emphasizing God's focus upon Israel and Jerusalem. This is why the passage immediately offers the context and the focal point of this period.

*Daniel 9:24 Seventy weeks are determined upon **thy people** and upon **thy holy city**.*

The focus of all of Daniel's Seventy Weeks is upon *thy people* (Israel) and *thy holy city* (Jerusalem). God's focus is certainly *not* upon Washington, D.C., Mecca, or any other city! All eyes are squarely upon Jerusalem. Additionally, the focus is not upon the Church or the Gentiles! It is not even upon the Muslims. God's focus and that of the world will be upon the little nation of Israel and His chosen people. The only churches left here on earth will be the false church described in Revelation chapter 18 and one similar to *"the church in the wilderness" (Acts 7:38).*

Seventy weeks (of years) are determined upon Israel with the first sixty-nine weeks (of years) having already been accomplished. That's 483 years with yet seven years (or one week of years) remaining in the future. During Daniel's future Seventieth Week (like the first sixty-nine weeks of years), God's attention focuses directly upon His people Israel.

> Seventy weeks (of years) are determined upon Israel with the first sixty-nine weeks (of years) having already been accomplished.

Verse 25 follows the seven purposes stated in verse 24 by providing some definite points or demarcations for determining the timing for all seventy weeks of years. The angel Gabriel admonishes Daniel:

*Daniel 9:25 **Know therefore and understand**, that from the going forth of the commandment to restore and to build Jerusalem unto the Messiah the Prince shall be **seven weeks, and threescore and two weeks**.*

The seven weeks and threescore and two weeks (of years) combine to equal 483 years. The starting point is easy to pinpoint by taking note that Daniel says this period starts from *"the going forth of the commandment to restore and to build Jerusalem"* and continues *"unto the Messiah the Prince."* Some confusion ensues because the Bible records four instances of decrees issued. The first three are found in the book of Ezra with the final one in Nehemiah.

- *Ezra 1:1-4* Cyrus (536 BC)
- *Ezra 6:7-12* Darius (519 BC)

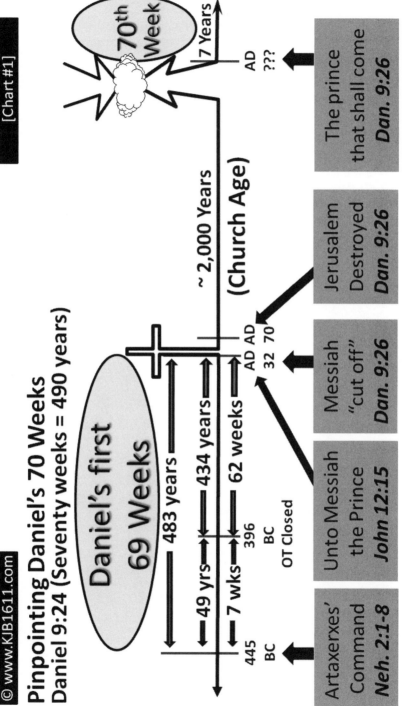

© www.KJB1611.com

Pinpointing Daniel's 70 Weeks
Daniel 9:24 (Seventy weeks = 490 years)

[Chart #1]

- *Ezra 7:11-26* Artaxerxes (458 BC)
- *Nehemiah 2:1-8* Artaxerxes (445 BC)

Daniel's prophecy refers to the final commandment to build or re-build Jerusalem issued by Artaxerxes to Nehemiah. Ussher's chronology places this time at 445 BC using our Gregorian calendar (and not Israel's lunar calendar). Converting the solar calendar to the lunar calendar reveals the time frame within the scriptural delineations. When the Bible says: *"from the going forth of the commandment to restore and to build Jerusalem,"* western history pinpoints the year as 445 BC. The Bible provides the end point of the first sixty-nine weeks as:

> *Daniel 9:25 . . . unto the Messiah the Prince shall be seven weeks, and threescore and two weeks: . . .*

Daniel tells us that the seven weeks and sixty-two weeks of years totalling 483 years continued *"unto the Messiah the Prince."* This prophetic fulfillment took place when the Lord Jesus Christ rode into Jerusalem as the Prince of Israel *(Zechariah 9:9, Luke 19:38)*. At that time, Christ fulfilled the prophecy of Zechariah and revealed Himself as the future King of Israel *(Matthew 21:5)*.

Daniel's prophecy then continues as it reveals the next point of demarcation as Christ's crucifixion that took place after these combined years. The Bible says that Messiah will be *"cut off"* AFTER the second period of sixty-two weeks of years which found its fulfillment in AD 32.

> *Daniel 9:26 And **after** threescore and two weeks **shall Messiah be cut off**, but not for himself.*

Obviously, Christ's crucifixion takes place at the conclusion of these sixty-nine weeks of years. The Bible confirms that He was cut off *"not for himself"* but *"for the sins of the whole world"* *(1 John 2:2)*. Daniel then identifies a second prince, which is not Jesus Christ, whose people destroy Jerusalem (which happened in AD 70).

> Christ's crucifixion takes place at the conclusion of these sixty-nine weeks of years.

> *Daniel 9:26 [A]nd the people of **the prince that shall come** shall destroy the city.*

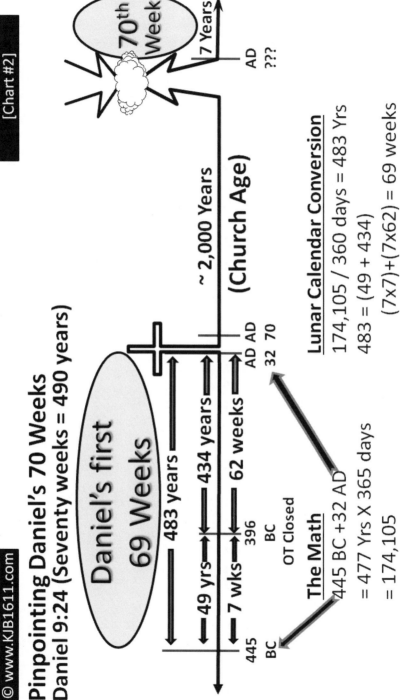

[Chart #2]

Pinpointing Daniel's 70 Weeks
Daniel 9:24 (Seventy weeks = 490 years)

Daniel's first 69 Weeks

70th Week

~2,000 Years (Church Age)

7 Years

AD ???

483 years
434 years
49 yrs
62 weeks
7 wks
445 BC
396 BC OT Closed
AD 32 AD 70

The Math
445 BC +32 AD
= 477 Yrs X 365 days
= 174,105

Lunar Calendar Conversion
174,105 / 360 days = 483 Yrs
483 = (49 + 434)
(7x7)+(7x62) = 69 weeks

Let's Do Some Math (Chart #2)

The split between the seven weeks and the sixty-two weeks reveals that the seven weeks (or the first forty-nine years) span from 445 BC to 396 BC. History reveals that the end point of this first set of years pinpoints the closing of the Old Testament Canon (about four centuries prior to Christ's birth). At that time, all thirty-nine books of the Old Testament were completed with no further recorded prophecy or revelation from God until Jesus shows up.

These forty-nine years (from 396 BC) were followed by 434 years which spanned up until the time that Christ triumphantly rode into Jerusalem in AD 32 as the Prince of Israel. Combining the years from 445 BC to AD 32 equates to 477 years (445 + 32 = 477). It is important to again emphasize that this computation uses the dates from the Gregorian calendar which utilizes a 365-day year equalling 174,105 days. However, the Bible months equal a consistent 30 days. Dividing this total number of days by 360 days converts the time into the Jewish lunar years which equals the 483 prophesied years (that is the 49 years plus the 434 years). This equals the sixty-nine weeks of years foretold by Daniel from Artaxerxes' command concerning Jerusalem up until Christ's riding into Jerusalem *(John 12:15)*.

The first sixty-nine weeks of years span from 445 BC on our calendar up until the events just prior to the crucifixion of Jesus Christ in AD 32. From the same passage in Daniel chapter 9, we know there remains one week of years to be fulfilled in the future. This last seven years will start after the Rapture of the Church and has been commonly referred to as Daniel's Seventieth Week. The reason the Bible refers to forty-two months, 1,260 days, or time, time, and half a time is because everything in that last seven-year period hinges upon what takes place at the midpoint. At that point, Satan is cast out of Heaven *(Revelation 12:9)*. The covenant is broken ending the daily sacrifice. The two witnesses start their ministry which lasts one half of the Seventieth Week *(Revelation 11:3)*. The next appendix will delve into the specifics of the Seventieth Week.

> This last seven years will start after the Rapture of the Church and has been commonly referred to as Daniel's Seventieth Week.

Charting Daniel's 70th Week

Appendix #2

Scripture reveals that the Seventy Weeks in Daniel chapter 9 apply directly to Israel with no part applying to the Church. As we delve into the significance of Daniel's Seventieth Week, keep in mind that many of the false teachings concerning this Week revolve around usurping God's future dealings with Israel.

It is both unwise and heretical to misrepresent God's intentions toward Israel. For this reason, the Bible nowhere teaches or condones any type of Replacement Theology (or

> Scripture reveals that the Seventy Weeks in Daniel chapter 9 apply directly to Israel with no part applying to the Church....It is both unwise and heretical to misrepresent God's intentions toward Israel.

Supersessionism). Yet, stealing or ignoring Israel's future (whether blessings or cursings) has been progressively increasing during the last few generations. Historically, this heretical philosophy gave the world the Nazi holocaust and has more recently inflamed the Muslim desire for Israel's extermination. This is why it is imperative to understand that each of Daniel's Seventy Weeks directly points to *thy people* (the Jews) and *thy holy city* (Jerusalem).

> **Daniel 9:24** *Seventy weeks are determined upon **thy people** and upon **thy holy city**, to finish the transgression, and to make an end of sins, and to make reconciliation for iniquity, and to bring in everlasting righteousness, and to seal up the vision and prophecy, and to anoint the most Holy.*

After the passage identifies the target audience (both the people and the place), Gabriel delineates the seven purposes of this time period. These purposes are:

1) to finish the transgression, and

2) to make an end of sins, and

3) to make reconciliation for iniquity, and

4) to bring in everlasting righteousness, and

5) to seal up the vision and

6) (to seal up the) prophecy, and

7) to anoint the most Holy

Each point could be addressed extensively, but honing in on the third purpose involving reconciliation frames the entire context of Daniel's Seventy Weeks. Christians are *not* waiting until a future time to be reconciled to God. Christians are already reconciled in Christ Jesus and in need of no further reconciliation *(Romans 5:10; 2 Corinthians 5:18; Colossians 1:21)*.

Israel's Future Reconciliation

Israel, on the other hand, awaits its future national reconciliation. This simple truth exposes one of the key challenges faced by those attempting to apply any part of Daniel's Seventy Weeks to the Church Age or to Christians in general. The Christian's reconciliation takes place fully at salvation.

The nation of Israel, however, is a much different story. When Christ came to earth, Israel rejected their Messiah. Israel's individual and national rejection triggered the deferral of Daniel's Seventieth Week by almost two millennia. During this period, God parenthetically placed the Church Age into time. As such, the Lord has been working with and through the Church for almost 2,000 years now. Even with God's attention clearly focussed upon the Church for almost two millennia, Paul used the present tense to write about God's covenant with Israel attesting to its future fulfillment *(Romans 11:26-27)*. Israel's reconciliation simply follows the Church's departure as one of the seven purposes of Daniel's Seventy Weeks. If Christians remain in need of reconciliation, then the Bible contains serious contradictions.

With sixty-nine of the seventy weeks of years historically past, the seven expressed purposes await their fulfillment during Daniel's Seventieth Week. With this in mind, it should be no surprise that all eyes are prophetically upon this unfulfilled event. The final week (the seven years yet future) begins with a prince (not the Prince) confirming a false covenant with "many" promising seven years of religious peace and peaceful existence.

Daniel 9:27a *And he shall* **confirm the covenant** *with many* **for one week***.*

The Key to Understanding the End Times

Providentially, Daniel chapter 9 provides *the key* for how Bible students can know for sure Daniel's Seventieth Week remains entirely in the future. The false prince will confirm his covenant with Israel for seven years. Without this confirmation of the covenant, no part of Daniel's Seventieth Week could have taken place yet. The first sixty-nine weeks ended just prior to the crucifixion of Jesus Christ. This ending was followed by God parenthetically placing the Church Age into time. The Church Age has now lasted for approximately 2,000 years and will close with the Blessed Hope (or the Rapture of the Church).

> The Church Age has now lasted for approximately 2,000 years and will close with the Blessed Hope (or the Rapture of the Church).

Though the prince (of verse 26) confirms his covenant with Israel for a full seven years, the Bible says that he will break that covenant and cause the sacrifices to cease.

Daniel 9:27b *[A]nd* **in the midst of the week** *he shall cause the sacrifice and the oblation to cease.*

In the midst of this final week of years—the seven-year period, the prince (again, not the Prince) will reveal his true intentions. The Bible repeatedly refers to this pivotal event in *Daniel 11:31, Daniel 12:11, Matthew 24:15,* and *Mark 13:14* as the *"abomination of desolation."* We know it will take place in the midst of the week and most likely at the midway point. This is the reason for so many designations for half of the week of years: 1,260 days; time, times, and half a time (*time* equalling one year); and forty-two months. Everything during that seven-year period hinges upon this key event at the end midpoint.

The Daily Jewish Sacrifice (Chart #3)

When Daniel's Seventieth Week begins, it will reintroduce a daily Jewish sacrifice. Scripturally, we can pinpoint precisely both the beginning and the interruption of these sacrifices. Discovering the sacrifice's conclusion is easiest for the scripture plainly states that at the midpoint of the week, the prince will *"cause the sacrifice and the oblation to cease."* We can then pinpoint when the sacrifice *begins* by using another time element provided—the 2,300 days. For now, we must simply recognize (1) that the covenant starts the clock for Daniel's Seventieth Week, (2) then follows the building of the temple which could take approximately seven months to complete, (3) the daily sacrifice ends with the abomination of desolation, and (4) from that point forward the Gentiles will *"tread under foot"* the holy city for forty-two months (3½ years).

> This is the reason for so many designations for half of the week of years: 1,260 days; time, times, and half a time (*time* equalling one year); and forty-two months. Everything during that seven-year period hinges upon this key event at the end midpoint.

> **Revelation 11:2** *But the court which is without the temple leave out, and measure it not; for it is given unto the **Gentiles**: and **the holy city shall they** (the Gentiles) **tread under foot forty and two months.***

This treading of the holy city (Jerusalem) under foot for forty-two months equates to the last half of Daniel's Seventieth Week. (The forty-two months equals 1,260 days using the biblical thirty day per month lunar calendar.)

The Day of the Lord/The Day of Christ

Matthew further establishes the end point for this event at the introduction of the Day of the Lord when it says that before that great and terrible day, the sun and the moon shall be darkened. It is important

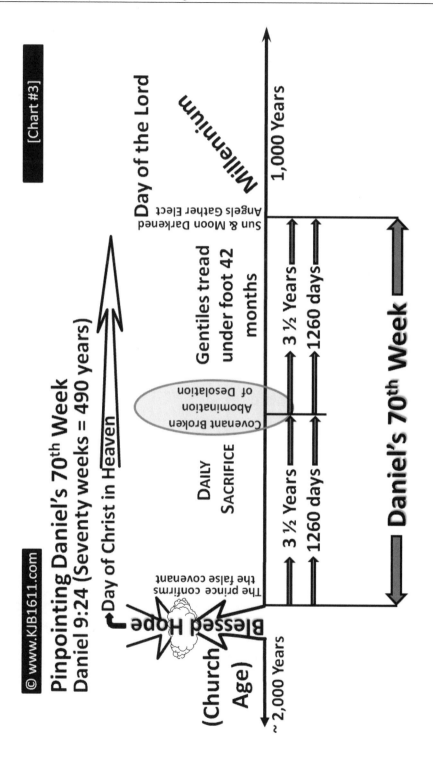

[Chart #3]

© www.KJB1611.com

Pinpointing Daniel's 70th Week
Daniel 9:24 (Seventy weeks = 490 years)

Day of Christ in Heaven

Day of the Lord

Millennium

1,000 Years

Sun & Moon Darkened
Angels Gather Elect

Gentiles tread under foot 42 months

Covenant Broken
Abomination of Desolation

DAILY SACRIFICE

3 ½ Years
1260 days

3 ½ Years
1260 days

Daniel's 70th Week

The prince confirms the false covenant

Blessed Hope

(Church Age)

~ 2,000 Years

to emphasize that the *Day of the Lord* does NOT begin on earth until after the sun and the moon are darkened toward the end of Daniel's Seventieth Week. This day, according to Second Peter, spans a thousand years and begins at the end of the Tribulation continuing throughout the Millennium and into the destruction of the heaven and earth *(2 Peter 3:10, Revelation 21:1)*.

Before the Day of the Lord, the Bible says that the Lord is going to send His angels to gather His elect *(Isaiah 45:4; Matthew 24:31)*. The elect certainly cannot be the Church because by then the Church has been absent from earth for almost seven years.

Lot in Genesis offers a poignant example of this gathering as he was supernaturally protected from the judgment to come upon the earth by the angels sent down to gather him and his family. The angels came down from Heaven and grabbed their hands, yanking them out of the city just before its destruction *(Luke 17:29-30)*. Likewise, the angels will gather the elect for protection just prior to the Lord's return. In fact, the Bible makes a clear distinction between the two gatherings by stating that Christ sends His angels for the elect in Matthew chapter 24 while the Lord HIMSELF descends for His body *(1 Thessalonians 4:16)*. It is equally important to note that the gathering of the Church commences *the Day of Christ* in Heaven *(2 Thessalonians 2:2; Philippians 1:6, 10, Philippians 2:16)*.

> [T]he Bible makes a clear distinction between the two gatherings by stating that Christ sends His angels for the elect in Matthew chapter 24 while the Lord HIMSELF descends for His body *(1 Thessalonians 4:16)*.

The Extra Days (Chart #4)

The 1,290 Days: The abomination of desolation (the hinge upon which Daniel's Seventieth Week hangs) takes place at the midpoint sandwiched between two equal three and one-half year periods (or 1,260 days or forty-two months). Daniel chapter 12, however, introduces another number of days which equates to an additional thirty days beyond Daniel's Seventieth Week.

*Daniel 12:11 And from the time that the daily sacrifice shall be taken away, and the abomination that maketh desolate set up, there shall be **a thousand two hundred and ninety days.***

Why the additional thirty days beyond the end of the 1,260 days? Keep in mind that the temple's desecration at the midpoint necessitates a cleansing. This cleansing takes place following the end of the Seventy Weeks.

The 1,335 Days: Verse 12 also mentions one more time frame—the 1,335 days. This time likely encompasses the judgment of the nations *(Matthew 25:31-46)*.

*Daniel 12:12 Blessed is he that waiteth, and cometh to **the thousand three hundred and five and thirty days.***

The 2,300 Days: Daniel chapter 8 references the most commonly misunderstood and misapplied prophetic time period—the 2,300 days *(Daniel 8:13-14)*! The resolution for understanding its coverage comes from two features mentioned. First, that the full 2,300 days is fully encapsulated within Daniel's Seventieth Week. Secondly, that the period consists of three interrelated elements:

> Daniel chapter 8 references the most commonly misunderstood and misapplied prophetic time period...the full 2,300 days is fully encapsulated within Daniel's Seventieth Week.

- the daily sacrifice from start to finish
- the transgression of desolation (aka the abomination of desolation)
- the Gentiles treading underfoot the sanctuary for forty-two months

Defined Beginning and Ending Points

The 2,300 days begins at the commencement of the daily sacrifice during the Seventieth Week. It does not end *"until the times of the Gentiles be fulfilled"* *(Luke 21:24)* at the close of the second half of Daniel's Seventieth Week *(Revelation 11:2)*. The question introducing this unique period clues the reader into the three elements combined to span the entire 2,300 days.

Daniel 8:13a *Then I heard one saint speaking, and another saint said unto that certain saint which spake,* **How long shall be the vision concerning the daily sacrifice?**

Carefully read the question for exactly what it says without any preconceived notions! The first element of the vision concerns the length of the vision concerning the daily sacrifice which provides the starting point for the 2,300 days. We must mathematically back into the starting point. The scripture confirms that the daily sacrifice **ceases** *"in the midst of the week"* **(*Daniel 9:27*)** by what the Bible refers to as the *"abomination of desolation."* This 2,300-day vision refers to this event as the *"transgression of desolation."*

Daniel 8:13b *. . . and* **the transgression of desolation,** *to give both the sanctuary and the host to be trodden under foot?*

Because the vision of the 2,300 days mentions the sanctuary being trodden under foot, we know the precise end point of the vision from the facts provided in Revelation chapter 12. The next verse tells us *how long* (1) the daily sacrifice, (2) the abomination of desolation, and (3) the Gentiles treading upon the sanctuary lasts—2,300 days all together—followed by the sanctuary being cleansed after Daniel's Seventieth Week ends.

Daniel 8:14 *And he said unto me,* **Unto two thousand and three hundred days;** *then shall the sanctuary be cleansed.*

What does the 2,300 days (or 6 1/3-year period) encompass? The inquiry reveals that it commences from the beginning of *the daily sacrifice* up through *the transgression of desolation*—the midpoint of the seven years—through the forty-two months that the *sanctuary and the host* (is) *to be trodden under foot.*

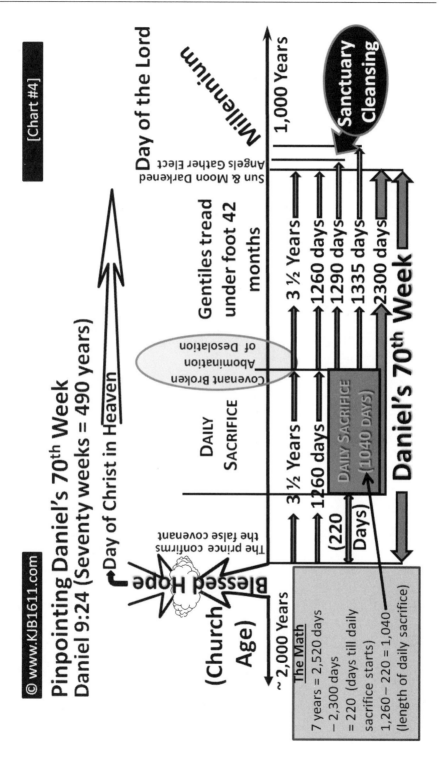

[Chart #4]

© www.KJB1611.com

Pinpointing Daniel's 70th Week
Daniel 9:24 (Seventy weeks = 490 years)

Day of Christ in Heaven

Blessed Hope

(Church Age)

~2,000 Years

The prince confirms the false covenant

DAILY SACRIFICE

3 ½ Years

1260 days

(220 Days)

DAILY SACRIFICE (1040 DAYS)

Covenant Broken
Abomination of Desolation

Gentiles tread under foot 42 months

3 ½ Years
1260 days
1290 days
1335 days
2300 days

Daniel's 70th Week

Day of the Lord

Sun & Moon Darkened
Angels Gather Elect

Millennium

1,000 Years

Sanctuary Cleansing

The Math

7 years = 2,520 days
− 2,300 days
= 220 (days till daily sacrifice starts)

1,260 − 220 = 1,040 (length of daily sacrifice)

Do the Math . . .

Since the full seven-year period encompasses exactly 2,520 days (1,260 + 1,260), subtracting the 2,300 days from the total period leaves 220 days remaining. This period of 7 1/3 months allows for the building of the temple along with the preparations necessary for the daily sacrifice to begin. This reveals that the seven-year covenant which follows the Rapture of the Church will begin with 220 days of preparation before the daily sacrifice can start. The daily sacrifice continues up until the midway point (or the abomination of desolation) when the temple is desecrated. At that time, the man of sin *"sitteth in the temple of God, shewing himself that he is God"* *(2 Thessalonians 2:4).*

> It is important to note that at the halfway point of the Week, Satan is cast out of heaven because the Bible says that he persecutes *the woman* (Israel) for time, times, and half a time *(Revelation 12:13-14; Daniel 7:25, Daniel 12:7)* or 3½ years.

Most likely, the man of sin will sacrifice something on the altar thus polluting the temple and the sanctuary *(Daniel 11:31).* It is important to note that at the halfway point of the Week, Satan is cast out of Heaven because the Bible says that he persecutes *the woman* (Israel) for time, times, and half a time *(Revelation 12:13-14; Daniel 7:25, Daniel 12:7)* or 3½ years.

Recapping the Numbers

Daniel's Seventieth Week commences when the prince confirms a false covenant for seven years. Approximately 220 days later, the daily sacrifices begin which last about 1,040 days until the sanctuary's desecration at the midpoint of Daniel's Seventieth Week. Satan causes this abomination after he is cast from heaven to earth where he persecutes Israel for 3½ years. At this same point, the Gentiles tread the sanctuary under foot for forty-two months.

When Jesus returns, He deals with the Devil, cleanses the temple, judges the nations, and establishes His Kingdom. These last few events take place toward the very end of the Seventieth Week and during the seventy-five days following.

Common Teaching Concerning "the Restrainer"

Appendix #3

Most of the Pre-tribulation teachers have taught or are teaching that God's Spirit restrains the revelation of the Man of Sin. While this may be true as a matter of timing, the Church's removal is not the impetus for the revealing of the Man of Sin. What follows is the common teaching that seems plausible until the timing of the removal of the restrainer is taken into account.

> *2 Thessalonians 2:7 For the mystery of iniquity doth already work: only he who now letteth will let, **until he be taken out of the way.***

It is true that the mystery of iniquity will not be fully revealed until after the Spirit-indwelt believers are taken out of the way. After all, believers are indwelt with someone greater than the *god of this world (2 Corinthians 4:4).*

> *1 John 4:4 Ye are of God, little children, and have overcome them: because **greater is he that is in you, than he that is in the world.***

For this reason and others, Pre-tribulationists commonly teach that when Spirit-indwelt believers disappear from the earth, it will cause a spiritual shift. Once those indwelt with God's Spirit depart on a mass scale, the present restraints upon this world will be loosed. The Devil's "christ" will be unveiled and the world will be deceived. This man will be the false christ of the cults and the deceived: the 12th Imam (or Mahdi) of Islam, the reincarnated Buddha of the Buddhists, the reborn Krishna of the Hindus, the portrayed effeminate christs found in most paintings, and the Jews' deceiving messiah.

The teaching, though not completely accurate, should be clarified. It is not simply the believers who are hindering Satan, but the ministry of the Spirit of God within believers! The context of Second Thessalonians is all about the revelation of the Man of Sin *(2 Thessalonians 2:3)* and the fact that he is NOW being withheld from his revelation *(2 Thessalonians 2:6)* by the Spirit-indwelled believers on this earth. Once the work of the Comforter (of reproving the world of sin, righteousness, and judgment) ceases, that Wicked one can be revealed *(2 Thessalonians 2:8)*.

After the Rapture of the Church, that *Wicked* one, Satan's seed *(Genesis 3:15)* shall be revealed in all his "glory." He is called the Antichrist because he is the antithesis of all that is God. The Lord Jesus Christ was the visible image of the invisible God *(Colossians 1:15)* and if you had seen Him, you had seen the Father *(John 14:9)*. The Antichrist will be the visible expression of the invisible Devil with the Beast as the bodily manifestation of Satan.

The Incarnate Christ Restrained the Coming Comforter

Though the timing is wrong, there is further precedent for those who have taught that the restrainer is the Spirit of God. Jesus foretold of the Comforter coming with a particular ministry as a result of indwelling the Church Age believers. Once believers are removed with the indwelling Comforter, His peculiar Church Age ministry and work will cease to function. Of course, the Spirit of God was omnipresent before indwelling believers and will remain omnipresent after the removal of Church Age believers. He will still be present on the earth after the Rapture, but when millions disappear, His work during the last two millennia of reproving the world of sin, righteousness, and judgment will come to a close.

> *John 16:7 Nevertheless I tell you the truth; It is expedient for you that I go away: **for if I go not away, the Comforter will not come unto you**; but if I depart, I will send him unto you. And when he is come, **he will reprove the world of sin, and of righteousness, and of judgment:***

According to scripture, Jesus hindered the Comforter from coming. Once Jesus had "go[ne] *away*," the Comforter could come with His special ministry and purpose. What is keeping Satan from being fully revealed? The common teaching is that it is Holy Ghost-indwelt believers. While this may be true in part, the chronology points to someone else. The text reveals the other party and lacks the apparent contradictions.

Compare the Last Days

Appendix #4

The last days of the Church Age—men will be:

- Lovers of their own selves *(2 Timothy 3:2)*
- Covetous *(2 Timothy 3:2)*
- Boasters *(2 Timothy 3:2)*
- Proud *(2 Timothy 3:2)*
- Blasphemers *(2 Timothy 3:2)*
- Disobedient to parents *(2 Timothy 3:2)*
- Unthankful *(2 Timothy 3:2)*
- Unholy *(2 Timothy 3:2)*
- Without natural affection *(2 Timothy 3:3)*
- Trucebreakers *(2 Timothy 3:3)*
- False accusers *(2 Timothy 3:3)*
- Incontinent *(2 Timothy 3:3)*
- Fierce *(2 Timothy 3:3)*
- Despisers of those that are good *(2 Timothy 3:3)*
- Traitors (*2 Timothy 3:4)*
- Heady *(2 Timothy 3:4)*
- Highminded *(2 Timothy 3:4)*
- Lovers of pleasures *(2 Timothy 3:4)*

The last days for Jews and unsaved Gentiles—will be marked by:

- Deceivers coming in the name of Christ *(Matthew 24:5)*
- War *(Matthew 24:6)*
- Famines *(Matthew 24:7)*
- Pestilences *(Matthew 24:7)*
- Earthquakes *(Matthew 24:7)*
- The gospel of the Kingdom *(Matthew 24:14)*

- The abomination of desolation *(Matthew 24:15)*
- Hoping that they do not need to flee on the Sabbath *(Matthew 24:20)*

The problems faced in the last days of the Church Age are spiritual in manifestation, whereas, the problems faced in the last days for the Jews and unsaved Gentiles are physical in nature. Notice that it was Jewish disciples who asked for the "sign" of the Lord's coming. The church of God needs no signs to mark the coming of Christ.

*1 Corinthians 1:22 For **the Jews require a sign,** and the Greeks seek after wisdom:*

Changing Apostasy to Departure

Appendix #5

by Doug Stauffer

It is never right to change God's word or to privately interpret scripture. Some Pre-tribulation teachers wishfully want the Bible to reference Rapture in *2 Thessalonians 2:3* rather than an apostasy or *"falling away."* They believe that if the Bible simply read *departure* (hopefully signifying the Rapture) this would bolster their Pre-tribulation stance. The problem is that God doesn't need our help to prove His teachings and never intended the Greek, Latin, or English to signify Rapture in this particular verse when it mentioned a falling away (or departure in pre-King James editions like the Geneva Bible, etc.).

> This word [departure] may have been appropriate until the English language developed its deeper and richer vocabulary during the late 1500s to the early 1600s.

The confusion began with Jerome's corrupt Latin Vulgate (AD 408) which translated the Greek word *apostasia* in verse 3 into the Latin *discessio* meaning *departure*. Many of the English pre-King James Bible texts followed suit using *departure* which could be construed through a forced meaning into the text as departing at the Rapture rather than simply a *departure* from the faith (or apostasy) as it does in other passages.

For instance, *departure* was used in the Wycliff Bible (1382) translated from the (Old) Latin which influenced the Tyndale (1525), Coverdale (1535), and Geneva (1560) Bibles to follow suit. This word may have been appropriate until the English language developed its deeper and richer vocabulary during the late 1500s to the early 1600s.

Interestingly, God never leaves the Bible student in the dark and without understanding. These earlier translations incorporated the word *departure* because of the influence of Jerome's Latin Vulgate and because it was an acceptable meaning during a time when English was still in its developmental infancy. However, each of these translations also consistently used depart from the faith in *1 Timothy 4:1* signifying apostasy (as does the King James Bible today). The translators prior to the King James Bible did not incorporate the word *departure* to signify the Rapture in 2 Thessalonians chapter 3 but to signify an apostasy from the faith.

The King James Bible during the height of the English language used a phrase that gives no wiggle room for misunderstanding. The end-times would truly be a Laodicean time caused by a lukewarm and ineffective Church. The English language from Wycliff to the Geneva Bibles was far from the richness that would be found during the early 1600s when the King James Bible was completed. Furthermore, the Greek word *apostasia* means apostasy, not a departure at the Rapture.

The Apostasy or Departing

Appendix #6

by Doug Stauffer

People frequently ask my thoughts (DS) concerning the English editions of the Bible that preceded the King James Bible, specifically why the Geneva Bible was "replaced." The purpose for the questions usually revolves around why the King James Bible (KJB) supposedly usurped the prominence of the Geneva and its predecessors. I generally begin by assuring the inquirer that the Geneva Bible was far superior to all of the English versions prior to its publication and rightfully superseded all of the earlier versions.

I point out that the King James Bible is also far superior to the Geneva and rightfully superseded it. Yet, many people also want to know what justification existed for the KJB to have replaced the Geneva Bible in America and around the world? The answer is quite simple, but first some groundwork.

After considerable research, I determined to provide those seeking the truth with a brief explanation as to why the King James Bible replaced the Geneva Bible. This very brief analysis primary focuses on *one word* in the Geneva Bible though this study could have covered a wide spectrum of words, each with similar outcomes. This study reveals what took place once English had reached its apex in the early 1600s. At the time of the publication of the Geneva Bible, history reveals that the English language was still rapidly developing. It had not reached its precipice of grandeur. In fact, English would not reach that milestone until four decades after the Geneva's translation and publication in 1560.

I combine the research of the Geneva Bible along with another study concerning the meaning of *falling away* as found in *2 Thessalonians*

2:3 because both subjects are interrelated. We begin by considering the reading of the subject text from the King James Bible as compared alongside the Geneva Bible.

> *(KJB) 2 Thessalonians 2:3 Let no man deceive you by any means: for that day shall not come, except there come a **falling away** first, and that man of sin be revealed, the son of perdition;*

> *(Geneva) 2 Thessalonians 2:3 Let no man deceiue you by any meanes: for that day shall not come, except there come a **departing** first, and that that man of sinne be disclosed, euen the sonne of perdition,*

Take note of the difference between the *"falling away"* in the KJB and *"departing"* in the Geneva Bible. At this point, it is important to note that the Greek word translated *"falling away"* in the KJB and *"departing"* in the Geneva is αποστασια *(apostasia)*. For now, we'll postpone the discussion concerning the difference in reading between the King James Bible and its predecessor, but this important fact will be adequately addressed.

Unfortunately, far too many well-intentioned Pre-tribulation teachers desperately want the Geneva Bible to mean the physical departing that takes place at the Rapture rather than the spiritual apostasy as intended by the text. I understand their zeal for an additional proof text, but zeal at any level never justifies changing the word of God or ignoring known facts. Some of these men will admit that the departure terminology was skewed a bit due to the Latin origin.

The Latin translation rendered the Greek *apostasia* into the Latin word *discessio* which more easily translates *"departure"* than does the Greek. The Bible critic then pontificates that the King James translator's theology got in the way as they *"interpreted"* rather than *"translated"* the passage. This is a convenient accusation since it is directed against defenceless men dead for almost four centuries. The fact is that the KJB translators simply translated *apostasia* using its primary usage—apostasy from the faith.

Departing from the Faith

The best way to help define what *departing* meant when used by the Geneva translators would involve considering the context of how *depart* is used elsewhere in the scriptures in this 1560 edition. In both the Geneva as well as the KJB, it is easy to determine that *departing* can and frequently does refer to spiritual apostasy. For example, the context of First Timothy provides one example of how the verb *"will depart from,"* αποστησονται in context, refers to apostasy (i.e., a departure FROM THE FAITH).

> *(Geneva) 1 Timothy 4:1 Nowe the Spirit speaketh euidently, that in the latter times some shall **depart from the faith**, and shall giue heede vnto spirits of errour, and doctrines of deuils,*

First Timothy is not the sole example. In fact, there are two more occurrences where the Geneva's literal usage and explicit language refer to a departing or falling away—an apostasy from the faith. Here are the other two passages from the Geneva.

> *(Geneva) Luke 8:13 They on the rock are they, which, when they hear, receive the word with joy; and these have no root, which for a while believe, and in time of temptation **fall away**.*

> *(Geneva) Hebrews 3:12 Take heed, brethren, lest there be in any of you an evil heart of unbelief, in **departing from the living God**.*

Each of these three examples from the Geneva Bible refers to a spiritual departure from the faith (i.e., apostasy). Well-meaning teachers have broken their necks spiritually speaking by running to the Greek in order to help out our Pre-tribulation Rapture cause. This is both unnecessary and can be unscrupulous once aware of the underlying facts.

These Greek proponents don't tell you that even those who use the most well-known Greek Lexicon (Liddell-Scott-Jones [LSJ] Greek-English Lexicon) claim that LSJ only ventures a guess as to what the noun apostasia means because the noun only occurs twice in scripture. These teachers are dogmatic when it is convenient to take a stand against English translations. However, they show themselves as quite wishy-washy when they don't like the LSJ definitions. Why would they question the LSJ Lexicon's first definition? Because the first definition reads: *"defection, revolt, esp. in religious sense, rebellion against God, apostasy."* Now, that seems pretty straight forward, but they want to cause doubt because the second definition seems to support their position: *"departure, disappearance."* Remember, God does not need man's help!

But how does the lexicon determine the definition of a word? Keep in mind that the writers of lexicons have been consistently shown to be guilty of allowing their doctrinal biases cloud their characterizations of the Greek grammar. They are also dealing with a living language (English) which during the 1500s was in a heightened state of irregularity and flux. In other words, a misunderstanding of the meaning and context of *2 Thessalonians 2:3* could lead the lexicographer to define the Greek noun *apostasia* as a physical departure because the English language was far from settled during the period when the earliest English language translations came into existence.

The second and only other occurrence of the noun *apostasia* (other than *2 Thessalonians 2:3*) is found in in *Acts 21:21.* Acts chapter 21 states that Paul was accused of *"teaching all the Jews who are among the Gentiles to forsake [apostasia] Moses."* The Geneva Bible concurs with the later reading in the KJB.

> *(Geneva) Acts 21:21 Now they are informed of thee, that thou teachest all the Iewes, which are among the Gentiles, to **forsake** Moses, and sayest that they ought not to circumcise their sonnes, neither to liue after the customes.*

It is quite obvious that the *apostasia* of forsaking the Law of Moses does not mean to depart spatially. These Jews believed that a departure from Moses (which infers a forsaking of the Law) was abject apostasy. However, Acts chapter 21 actually helps define the subject passage in Second Thessalonians since there is no object expressed there, but there is one in Acts chapter 21.

Apostasia

Background: *apostasia* is a Greek compound word of *apo* which means "from" and *istemi* "stand." Thus, the core meaning of the Greek *apostasia* means *"away from"* or *"departure"* from truth. Neither of the two usages of the NOUN in 2 Thessalonians chapter 2 or Acts chapter 21 involves a spatial movement of any kind (i.e., a Rapture).

The verb from which the noun *apostasia* is supports the basic meaning of *departure*. The Greek word occurs in **verb form** a total of fifteen times in the New Testament with three of these referring to a departure from the faith discussed earlier. The remaining usages could infer a spatial departure, like departing from a room.

- In other settings, the word is used for departing from iniquity.

*2 **Timothy 2:19** Nevertheless the foundation of God standeth sure, having this seal, The Lord knoweth them that are his. And, Let every one that nameth the name of Christ **depart from iniquity.***

- departing from ungodly men

*1 **Timothy 6:5** Perverse disputings of men of corrupt minds, and destitute of the truth, supposing that gain is godliness: **from such withdraw thyself.***

- departing from the temple

***Luke 2:37** And she was a widow of about fourscore and four years, which **departed** not from the temple, but served God with fastings and prayers night and day.*

- departing from the body

2 Corinthians 12:8** For this thing I besought the Lord thrice, that it might **depart from me.

- and departing from persons

***Acts 12:10** When they were past the first and the second ward, they came unto the iron gate that leadeth unto the city; which opened to them of his own accord: and they went out, and passed on through one street; and forthwith the angel **departed** from him.*

***Luke 4:13** And when the devil had ended all the temptation, he **departed** from him for a season.*

Adding to the misapplication of the Greek usage by those trying to help out God, the point is also made that the seven major English translations of the Bible prior to the 1600s rendered the noun *apostasia* as either "departure" or "departing" in *2 Thessalonians 2:3*. They are as follows:

The Wycliffe Bible (1382): *No man disseyue you in ony manere. For but **dissencioun** come first, and the man of synne be schewid, the sonne of perdicioun,*

The Tyndale Bible (1525): *Let no ma deceave you by eny meanes for the lorde commeth not excepte ther come a **departynge** fyrst and that that synfnll man be opened ye sonne of perdicion*

The Coverdale Bible (1535): *Let noman disceaue you by eny meanes. For the LORDE commeth not, excepte the **departynge** come first, and that that Man of synne be opened, euen the sonne of perdicion,*

The Matthews Bible (1537): *Let no man deceyue you by any meanes, for the Lord commeth not, except there come a **departyng** first, and that, that sinful man be opened, the sonne of perdicyon*

The Great Bible (1538): *Let no man deceaue you by eny meanes, for the Lorde shall not come excepte ther come a **departynge** fyrst, and that that synfull man be opened, the sonne of perdicyon,*

The Geneva Bible (1560): *Let no man deceiue you by any meanes: for that day shall not come, except there come a **departing** first, and that that man of sinne be disclosed, euen the sonne of perdition,*

Interestingly, those who seek to place "blame" upon the King James Bible ignore the fact that it was the Bishop's Bible of 1568 that contained the reading prior to the King James. The reading changed because the English language was still developing and the Bishop's Bible followed the more precise conveyance of God's intent.

The Bishop's Bible (1568): *Let no man deceaue you by any meanes, for the Lorde shall not come excepte there come a **fallyng away** first, & that that man of sinne be reuealed, the sonne of perdition,*

Purified Seven Times

When I was teaching at a pastor's conference in Mindanao, Philippines, one of the pastors asked me a question concerning something that I had written in *One Book Stands Alone*. It dealt with the application of *Psalm 12:6-7* to the seven stage purification resulting in the King James as the seventh primary Greek to English translation with the first six specifically mentioned in the rules for the translators. He asked how the word of God could be purified seven times. It was an excellent question and really insightful and one in which the Lord provided the answer on the spot.

I told him that the problem with the versions prior to the King James Bible was not a problem with the word of God nor the translation process prior to 1611; the differences were attributable to the developmental level of the English language. In the early 1600s, the English language was at its height in purity, richness, and fullness. In 1560, the time of the Geneva Bible publication, the English language was at a much lower level with fewer words and thus a less rich vocabulary. We will consider one word in the Geneva Bible to prove this fact. It is the word "depart" with all of its variations. The variations of the word *depart* are found 469 times in 454 verses in the Geneva Bible.

Word/Phrase	Match Count
depart	160
departed	283
departedst	1
departeth	8
departing	13
departture	1
departure	3
Total 469	

The reason for a less expansive vocabulary prior to the early 1600s is directly attributable to the English language. This evolving language simply used the same word for what would later become a much deeper vocabulary. In order to illustrate the depth of the English language a mere forty years AFTER the Geneva Bible, a simple review of the 469 uses of *depart* and its six variations offers these **78 varied results** in the King James Bible: (1) went forth; (2) separate thyself; (3) separated themselves; (4) journeyed from; (5) send me away; (6) went his way; (7) went out; (8) absent; (9) we will be gone; (10) journeyed; (11) be gone; (12) leave; (13) let him go; (14) he removed; (15) go out; (16) journeying; (17) took; (18) set forward; (19) take your journey; (20) turned; (21) passed by; (22) turned myself; (23) remove; (24) very; (25) came forth; (26) passed; (27) Go and walk; (28) went; (29) Go; (30) severed himself; (31) marchest; (32) Went forth; (33) return from following after; (34) part; (35) removed; (36) gone about; (37) go well away; (38) turn aside; (39) gone up; (40) gone; (41) quite gone; (42) went forth; (43) go forth; (44) went away; (45) return; (46) went into; (47) separated; (48) gone back; (49) am gone; (50) err; (51) goeth forth; (52) taken away; (53) be satisfied; (54) be; (55) put away; (56) be removed; (57) Get you; (58) on his way; (59) fled; (60) revolted; (61) pass away; (62) go far off;

(63) get; (64) estranged; (65) separated himself; (66) alienated; (67) gone down; (68) pass; (69) went; (70) withdrew himself from; (71) goeth; (72) send…away; (73) decrease; (74) parted; (75) dismissed; (76) gotten; (77) falling away; (78) decease.

For those desiring additional concrete proof, here are some of the actual verses themselves with the changes highlighted. For example, the first instance shows that *"departed"* in the Geneva Bible was translated as *"went forth"* in 1611. [1]

1. (GB) departed = (KJB) went forth

*(Geneva) Genesis 11:31 Then Terah tooke Abram his sonne, and Lot the sonne of Haran, his sonnes sonne, and Sarai his daughter in lawe, his sonne Abrams wife: and they **departed** together from Vr of the Caldees, to goe into the land of Canaan, and they came to Haran, and dwelt there.*

*(KJB) Genesis 11:31 And Terah took Abram his son, and Lot the son of Haran his son's son, and Sarai his daughter in law, his son Abram's wife; and they **went forth** with them from Ur of the Chaldees, to go into the land of Canaan; and they came unto Haran, and dwelt there.*

2. (GB) depart = (KJB) separate thyself

*(Geneva) Genesis 13:9 Is not the whole land before thee? **depart** I pray thee from me: if thou wilt take the left hand, then I will goe to the right: or if thou goe to the right hand, then I will take the left.*

*(KJB) Genesis 13:9 Is not the whole land before thee? **separate thyself**, I pray thee, from me: if thou wilt take the left hand, then I will go to the right; or if thou depart to the right hand, then I will go to the left.*

3. (GB) departed = (KJB) separated themselves

*(Geneva) Genesis 13:11 Then Lot chose vnto him all the plaine of Iorden, and tooke his iourney from the East: and they **departed** the one from the other.*

---

[1] Again, this is not an issue of manuscripts or an issue of inferior translation by pre-1611 editions; it revolves around how a living language causes adaptation especially as it concerns translational issues. Fortunately, the English language was at its peak in the early 1600s. Unfortunately, the 20th and 21st centuries have experienced a dumbing down and degradation of this once richest of languages.

(KJB) Genesis 13:11 Then Lot chose him all the plain of Jordan; and Lot journeyed east: and they **separated themselves** the one from the other.

4. (GB) departed = (KJB) journeyed from

(Geneva) Genesis 20:1 Afterward Abraham **departed** thence toward the South countrey and dwelled betweene Cadesh and Shur, and soiourned in Gerar.

(KJB) Genesis 20:1 And Abraham **journeyed from** thence toward the south country, and dwelled between Kadesh and Shur, and sojourned in Gerar.

5. (GB) Let me depart = (KJB) Send me away

(Geneva) Genesis 24:54 Afterward they did eate & drinke, both he, and the men that were with him, and taried all night. and when they rose vp in the morning, he said, **Let me depart** vnto my master.

(KJB) Genesis 24:54 And they did eat and drink, he and the men that were with him, and tarried all night; and they rose up in the morning, and he said, **Send me away** unto my master.

6. (GB) departed = (KJB) went his way

(Geneva) Genesis 24:61 Then Rebekah arose, & her maydes, and rode vpon the camels, and followed the man. and the seruant tooke Rebekah, and **departed**.

(KJB) Genesis 24:61 And Rebekah arose, and her damsels, and they rode upon the camels, and followed the man: and the servant took Rebekah, and **went his way.**

7. (GB) departed = (KJB) went out

(Geneva) Genesis 28:10 Now Iaakob **departed** from Beer-sheba, and went to Haran,

(KJB) Genesis 28:10 And Jacob **went out** from Beersheba, and went toward Haran.

8. (GB) departed = (KJB) absent

(Geneva) Genesis 31:49 Also he called it Mizpah, because he said, The Lorde looke betweene me and thee, when we shalbe **departed** one from another,

*(KJB) Genesis 31:49 And Mizpah; for he said, The LORD watch between me and thee, when we are **absent** one from another.*

9. (GB) depart = (KJB) we will be gone

*(Geneva) Genesis 34:17 But if ye will not hearken vnto vs to be circumcised, then will we take our daughter and **depart**.*

*(KJB) Genesis 34:17 But if ye will not hearken unto us, to be circumcised; then will we take our daughter, and **we will be gone**.*

10. (GB) departed = (KJB) journeyed

*(Geneva) Genesis 35:16 Then they **departed** from Beth-el, and when there was about halfe a daies iourney of ground to come to Ephrath, Rahel trauailed, and in trauailing she was in perill.*

*(KJB) Genesis 35:16 And they **journeyed** from Bethel; and there was but a little way to come to Ephrath: and Rachel travailed, and she had hard labour.*

11. (GB) depart = (KJB) be gone

*(Geneva) Genesis 42:33 Then the Lord of the countrey sayde vnto vs, Hereby shal I knowe if ye be true men: Leaue one of your brethren with me, and take foode for the famine of your houses and **depart**,*

*(KJB) Genesis 42:33 And the man, the lord of the country, said unto us, Hereby shall I know that ye are true men; leave one of your brethren here with me, and take food for the famine of your households, and **be gone**:*

12. (GB) depart from = (KJB) leave

*(Geneva) Genesis 44:22 And we answered my lord, The childe can not **depart from** his father: for if he leaue his father, his father would die.*

*(KJB) Genesis 44:22 And we said unto my lord, The lad cannot **leave** his father: for if he should leave his father, his father would die.*

13. (GB) departed from him = (KJB) let him go

*(Geneva) Exodus 4:26 So he **departed from him**. Then she saide, O bloodie husbande (because of the circumcision)*

*(KJB) Exodus 4:26 So he **let him go***: then she said, A bloody husband thou art, because of the circumcision.

14. (GB) departed = (KJB) he removed

*(Geneva) Exodus 8:31 And the Lord did according to the saying of Moses, and the swarmes of flies **departed** from Pharaoh, from his seruants, and from his people, and there remained not one.*

*(KJB) Exodus 8:31 And the LORD did according to the word of Moses; and **he removed** the swarms of flies from Pharaoh, from his servants, and from his people; there remained not one.*

15. (GB) depart = (KJB) go out

*(Geneva) Exodus 11:8 And all these thy seruants shall come downe vnto me, and fal before me, saying, Get thee out, and all the people that are at thy feete, and after this will I **depart**. So he went out from Pharaoh very angry.*

*(KJB) Exodus 11:8 And all these thy servants shall come down unto me, and bow down themselves unto me, saying, Get thee out, and all the people that follow thee: and after that I will **go out**. And he went out from Pharaoh in a great anger.*

16. (GB) departure = (KJB) journeying

*(Geneva) Numbers 10:2 Make thee two trumpets of siluer: of an whole piece shalt thou make the, that thou mayest vse them for the assembling of the Congregation, and for the **departure** of the campe.*

*(KJB) Numbers 10:2 Make thee two trumpets of silver; of a whole piece shalt thou make them: that thou mayest use them for the calling of the assembly, and for the **journeying** of the camps.*

17. (GB) departed = (KJB) took

*(Geneva) Numbers 10:12 And ye children of Israel **departed** on their iourneys out of the desart of Sinai, & the cloud rested in the wildernesse of Paran.*

*(KJB) Numbers 10:12 And the children of Israel **took** their journeys out of the wilderness of Sinai; and the cloud rested in the wilderness of Paran.*

18. (GB) departed = (KJB) set forward

*(Geneva) Numbers 10:18 After, **departed** the standerd of the hoste of Reuben, according to their armies, and ouer his band was Elizur the sonne of Shedeur.*

*(KJB) Numbers 10:18 And the standard of the camp of Reuben **set forward** according to their armies: and over his host was Elizur the son of Shedeur.*

19. (GB) depart = (KJB) take your journey

*(Geneva) Deuteronomy 1:7 Turne you and **depart**, and goe vnto the mountaine of the Amorites, and vnto all places neere thereunto in the plaine, in the mountaine, or in the valley: both Southwarde, and to the Sea side, to the land of the Canaanites, and vnto Lebanon: euen vnto the great riuer, the riuer Perath.*

*(KJB) Deuteronomy 1:7 Turn you, and **take your journey**, and go to the mount of the Amorites, and unto all the places nigh thereunto, in the plain, in the hills, and in the vale, and in the south, and by the sea side, to the land of the Canaanites, and unto Lebanon, unto the great river, the river Euphrates.*

20. (GB) departed = (KJB) turned

*(Geneva) Deuteronomy 1:24 Who **departed**, and went vp into the mountaine, and came vnto the riuer Eshcol, and searched out the land.*

*(KJB) Deuteronomy 1:24 And they **turned** and went up into the mountain, and came unto the valley of Eshcol, and searched it out.*

21. (GB) departed = (KJB) passed by

*(Geneva) Deuteronomy 2:8 And when we were **departed** from our brethren the children of Esau which dwelt in Seir, through the way of the plaine, from Elath, and from Ezion-gaber, we turned and went by the way of the wildernes of Moab.*

*(KJB) Deuteronomy 2:8 And when we **passed by** from our brethren the children of Esau, which dwelt in Seir, through the way of the plain from Elath, and from Eziongaber, we turned and passed by the way of the wilderness of Moab.*

22. (GB) departed = (KJB) turned myself

(Geneva) Deuteronomy 10:5 And I departed, and came downe from the Mount, and put the Tables in the Arke which I had made: and there they be, as the Lorde commanded me.

(KJB) Deuteronomy 10:5 And I turned myself and came down from the mount, and put the tables in the ark which I had made; and there they be, as the LORD commanded me.

23. (GB) depart = (KJB) remove

(Geneva) Joshua 3:3 And commanded the people, saying, When ye see the Arke of the couenat of the Lord your God, and the Priestes of the Leuites bearing it, ye shall depart from your place, and goe after it.

(KJB) Joshua 3:3 And they commanded the people, saying, When ye see the ark of the covenant of the LORD your God, and the priests the Levites bearing it, then ye shall remove from your place, and go after it.

24. (GB) departed = (KJB) very

(Geneva) Joshua 3:16 Then the waters that came downe from aboue, stayed and rose vpon an heape and departed farre from the citie of Adam, that was beside Zaretan: but the waters that came downe towarde the Sea of the wildernes, euen the salt Sea, failed, and were cut off: so the people went right ouer against Iericho.

(KJB) Joshua 3:16 That the waters which came down from above stood and rose up upon an heap very far from the city Adam, that is beside Zaretan: and those that came down toward the sea of the plain, even the salt sea, failed, and were cut off: and the people passed over right against Jericho.

25. (GB) departed = (KJB) came forth

(Geneva) Joshua 9:12 This our bread we tooke it hote with vs for vittailes out of our houses, the day we departed to come vnto you: but nowe beholde, it is dried, and it is mouled.

(KJB) Joshua 9:12 This our bread we took hot for our provision out of our houses on the day we came forth to go unto you; but now, behold, it is dry, and it is mouldy:

26. (GB) departed = (KJB) passed

*(Geneva) Joshua 10:31 And Ioshua **departed** from Libnah, and all Israel with him vnto Lachish, and besieged it, and assaulted it.*

*(KJB) Joshua 10:31 And Joshua **passed** from Libnah, and all Israel with him, unto Lachish, and encamped against it, and fought against it:*

27. (GB) Depart, and goe = (KJB) Go and walk

*(Geneva) Joshua 18:8 Then the men arose, and went their way: and Ioshua charged them that went to describe the land, saying, **Depart, and goe** through the land, and describe it, and returne to me, that I may here cast lottes for you before the Lord in Shiloh.*

*(KJB) Joshua 18:8 And the men arose, and went away: and Joshua charged them that went to describe the land, saying, **Go and walk** through the land, and describe it, and come again to me, that I may here cast lots for you before the LORD in Shiloh.*

28. (GB) departed = (KJB) went

*(Geneva) Joshua 18:9 So the men **departed**, and passed through the lande, and described it by cities into seuen partes in a booke, and returned to Ioshua into the campe at Shiloh.*

*(KJB) Joshua 18:9 And the men **went** and passed through the land, and described it by cities into seven parts in a book, and came again to Joshua to the host at Shiloh.*

29. (GB) depart = (KJB) go

*(Geneva) Judges 1:25 And when hee had shewed them the waie into the citie, they smote the citie with the edge of the sworde, but they let the man and all his housholde **depart**.*

*(KJB) Judges 1:25 And when he shewed them the entrance into the city, they smote the city with the edge of the sword; but they let **go** the man and all his family.*

30. (GB) departed = (KJB) severed himself

*(Geneva) Judges 4:11 (Now Heber the Kenite, which was of the children of Hobab the father in lawe of Moses, was **departed** from the*

Kenites, and pitched his tent vntill the playne of Zaanaim, which is by Kedesh)

(KJB) Judges 4:11 Now Heber the Kenite, which was of the children of Hobab the father in law of Moses, had **severed himself** from the Kenites, and pitched his tent unto the plain of Zaanaim, which is by Kedesh.

31. (GB) deparedst = (KJB) marchedst

(Geneva) Judges 5:4 Lorde, when thou wentest out of Seir, when thou **departedst** out of the field of Edom, the earth trembled, and the heauens rained, the cloudes also dropped water.

(KJB) Judges 5:4 LORD, when thou wentest out of Seir, when thou **marchedst** out of the field of Edom, the earth trembled, and the heavens dropped, the clouds also dropped water.

32. (GB) departed = (KJB) went forth

(Geneva) Ruth 1:7 Wherefore shee **departed** out of the place where she was, and her two daughters in law with her, and they went on their way to returne vnto the land of Iudah.

(KJB) Ruth 1:7 Wherefore she **went forth** out of the place where she was, and her two daughters in law with her; and they went on the way to return unto the land of Judah.

33. (GB) depart from = (KJB) return from following after

(Geneva) Ruth 1:16 And Ruth answered, Intreate mee not to leaue thee, nor to **depart from** thee: for whither thou goest, I will goe: and where thou dwellest, I will dwell: thy people shall be my people, and thy God my God.

(KJB) Ruth 1:16 And Ruth said, Intreat me not to leave thee, or to **return from following after** thee: for whither thou goest, I will go; and where thou lodgest, I will lodge: thy people shall be my people, and thy God my God:

34. (GB) depart = (KJB) part

(Geneva) Ruth 1:17 Where thou diest, will I die, and there will I be buried. the Lord do so to me and more also, if ought but death **depart** thee and me.

*(KJB) Ruth 1:17 Where thou diest, will I die, and there will I be buried: the LORD do so to me, and more also, if ought but death **part** thee and me.*

35. (GB) departeth = (KJB) removed

*(Geneva) 1 Samuel 6:3 And they sayd, If you send away the Arke of the God of Israel, send it not away emptie, but giue vnto it a sinne offering: then shall ye be healed, and it shall be knowen to you, why his hand **departeth** not from you.*

*(KJB) 1 Samuel 6:3 And they said, If ye send away the ark of the God of Israel, send it not empty; but in any wise return him a trespass offering: then ye shall be healed, and it shall be known to you why his hand is not **removed** from you.*

36. (GB) departed = (KJB) gone about

*(Geneva) 1 Samuel 15:12 And when Samuel arose early to meete Saul in the morning, one tolde Samuel, saying, Saul is gone to Carmel: and beholde, he hath made him there a place, from whence he returned, and **departed**, and is gone downe to Gilgal.*

*(KJB) 1 Samuel 15:12 And when Samuel rose early to meet Saul in the morning, it was told Samuel, saying, Saul came to Carmel, and, behold, he set him up a place, and is **gone about**, and passed on, and gone down to Gilgal.*

37. (GB) depart free = (KJB) go well away

*(Geneva) 1 Samuel 24:19 For who shal finde his enemie, and let him **depart free**? wherefore the Lorde render thee good for that thou hast done vnto me this day.*

*(KJB) 1 Samuel 24:19 For if a man find his enemy, will he let him **go well away**? wherefore the LORD reward thee good for that thou hast done unto me this day.*

38. (GB) depart = (KJB) turn aside

*(Geneva) 2 Samuel 2:21 Then Abner said, Turne thee either to the right hande, or to the left, and take one of the yong men, and take thee his weapons: and Asahel would not **depart** from him.*

(KJB) 2 Samuel 2:21 And Abner said to him, Turn thee aside to thy right hand or to thy left, and lay thee hold on one of the young men, and take thee his armour. But Asahel would not **turn aside** from following of him.

39. (GB) departed = (KJB) gone up

(Geneva) 2 Samuel 2:27 And Ioab sayde, As God liueth, if thou haddest not spoken, surely euen in the morning the people had **departed** euery one backe from his brother.

(KJB) 2 Samuel 2:27 And Joab said, As God liveth, unless thou hadst spoken, surely then in the morning the people had **gone up** every one from following his brother.

40. (GB) departed = (KJB) gone

(Geneva) 2 Samuel 3:22 And beholde, the seruants of Dauid and Ioab came from the campe, and brought a great Pray with them (but Abner was not with Dauid in Hebron: for he had sent him away, and he **departed** in peace)

(KJB) 2 Samuel 3:22 And, behold, the servants of David and Joab came from pursuing a troop, and brought in a great spoil with them: but Abner was not with David in Hebron; for he had sent him away, and he was **gone** in peace.

41. (GB) departed = (KJB) quite gone

(Geneva) 2 Samuel 3:24 Then Ioab came to the King, and saide, What hast thou done? beholde, Abner came vnto thee, why hast thou sent him away, and he is **departed**?

(KJB) 2 Samuel 3:24 Then Joab came to the king, and said, What hast thou done? behold, Abner came unto thee; why is it that thou hast sent him away, and he is **quite gone**?

42. (GB) departed = (KJB) went forth

(Geneva) 2 Samuel 15:16 So the King **departed** and all his houshold after him, and the King left ten concubines to keepe the house.

(KJB) 2 Samuel 15:16 And the king **went forth**, and all his household after him. And the king left ten women, which were concubines, to keep the house.

43. (GB) depart = (KJB) go forth

(Geneva) 2 Kings 9:15 And King Ioram returned to bee healed in Izreel of the woundes, which the Aramites had giuen him, when hee fought with Hazael King of Aram) and Iehu sayde, If it be your mindes, let no man **depart** *and escape out of the citie, to goe and tell in Izreel.*

(KJB) 2 Kings 9:15 But king Joram was returned to be healed in Jezreel of the wounds which the Syrians had given him, when he fought with Hazael king of Syria.) And Jehu said, If it be your minds, then let none **go forth** *nor escape out of the city to go to tell it in Jezreel..*

44. (GB) departed = (KJB) went away

(Geneva) 2 Kings 12:18 And Iehoash King of Iudah tooke all the halowed thinges that Iehoshaphat, and Iehoram, and Ahaziah his fathers Kings of Iudah had dedicated, and that he himselfe had dedicated, and all the golde that was found in the treasures of the house of the Lord and in the Kings house, and sent it to Hazael King of Aram, and he **departed** *from Ierusalem.*

(KJB) 2 Kings 12:18 And Jehoash king of Judah took all the hallowed things that Jehoshaphat, and Jehoram, and Ahaziah, his fathers, kings of Judah, had dedicated, and his own hallowed things, and all the gold that was found in the treasures of the house of the LORD, and in the king's house, and sent it to Hazael king of Syria: and he **went away** *from Jerusalem.*

45. (GB) depart = (KJB) return

(Geneva) 2 Kings 18:14 Then Hezekiah King of Iudah sent vnto the King of Asshur to Lachish, saying, I haue offended: **depart** *from me, & what thou layest vpon me, I wil beare it. And the King of Asshur appoynted vnto Hezekiah King of Iudah three hudreth talents of siluer, & thirty talets of golde.*

(KJB) 2 Kings 18:14 And Hezekiah king of Judah sent to the king of Assyria to Lachish, saying, I have offended; **return** *from me: that which thou puttest on me will I bear. And the king of Assyria appointed unto Hezekiah king of Judah three hundred talents of silver and thirty talents of gold.*

46. (GB) departed = (KJB) went into

(Geneva) **1 Chronicles 6:15** *And Iehozadak* **departed** *when the Lord caried away into captiuitie Iudah and Ierusalem by the hand of Nebuchad-nezzar.*

(KJB) **1 Chronicles 6:15** *And Jehozadak* **went into** *captivity, when the LORD carried away Judah and Jerusalem by the hand of Nebuchadnezzar.*

47. (GB) departed = (KJB) separated

(Geneva) **Ezra 10:16** *And they of the captiuitie did so, & **departed**, euen Ezra a the Priest, & the men that were chiefe fathers to the familie of their fathers by name, and sate downe in the first day of the tenth moneth to examine the matter.*

(KJB) **Ezra 10:16** *And the children of the captivity did so. And Ezra the priest, with certain chief of the fathers, after the house of their fathers, and all of them by their names, were* **separated**, *and sat down in the first day of the tenth month to examine the matter.*

48. (GB) departed = (KJB) gone back

(Geneva) **Job 23:12** *Neyther haue I* **departed** *from the commandement of his lippes, and I haue esteemed the words of his mouth more then mine appointed foode.*

(KJB) **Job 23:12** *Neither have I* **gone back** *from the commandment of his lips; I have esteemed the words of his mouth more than my necessary food.*

49. (GB) depart = (KJB) am gone

(Geneva) **Psalm 109:23** *I* **depart** *like the shadowe that declineth, and am shaken off as the grashopper.*

*(KJB)***Psalm 109:23** *I* **am gone** *like the shadow when it declineth: I am tossed up and down as the locust.*

50. (GB) depart = (KJB) err

(Geneva) **Psalm 119:118** *Thou hast troden downe all them that* **depart** *from thy statutes: for their deceit is vaine.*

*(KJB)Psalm 119:118 Thou hast trodden down all them that **err** from thy statutes: for their deceit is falsehood.*

51. (GB) departeth = (KJB) goeth forth

*(Geneva) Psalm 146:4 His breath **departeth**, and he returneth to his earth: then his thoughtes perish.*

*(KJB) Psalm 146:4 His breath **goeth forth**, he returneth to his earth; in that very day his thoughts perish.*

52. (GB) departeth = (KJB) taken away

*(Geneva) Proverbs 4:16 For they can not sleepe, except they haue done euill, and their sleepe **departeth** except they cause some to fall.*

*(KJB) Proverbs 4:16 For they sleep not, except they have done mischief; and their sleep is **taken away**, unless they cause some to fall.*

53. (GB) depart = (KJB) be satisfied

*(Geneva) Proverbs 14:14 The heart that declineth, shall be saciate with his owne wayes: but a good man shall **depart** from him.*

*(KJB) Proverbs 14:14 The backslider in heart shall be filled with his own ways: and a good man shall **be satisfied** from himself.*

54. (GB) depart = (KJB) be

*(Geneva) Proverbs 22:5 Thornes and snares are in the way of the frowarde: but he that regardeth his soule, will **depart** farre from them.*

*(KJB) Proverbs 22:5 Thorns and snares are in the way of the froward: he that doth keep his soul shall **be** far from them.*

55. (GB) depart = (KJB) put away

*(Geneva) Ecclessiastes11:10 Therefore take away griefe out of thine heart, and cause euil to **depart** from thy flesh: for childehoode and youth are vanitie.*

*(KJB) Ecclesiastes 11:10 Therefore remove sorrow from thy heart, and **put away** evil from thy flesh: for childhood and youth are vanity.*

56. (GB) depart = (KJB) be removed

*(Geneva) Isaiah 22:25 In that day, sayeth the Lord of hostes, shall the naile, that is fastned in the sure place, **depart** and shall be broken, and fall: and the burden, that was vpon it, shall bee cut off: for the Lorde hath spoken it.*

*(KJB) Isaiah 22:25 In that day, saith the LORD of hosts, shall the nail that is fastened in the sure place **be removed**, and be cut down, and fall; and the burden that was upon it shall be cut off: for the LORD hath spoken it.*

57. (GB) Depart = (KJB) Get you

*(Geneva) Isaiah 30:11 **Depart** out of the way: go aside out of the path: cause the holy one of Israel to cease fro vs.*

*(KJB) Isaiah 30:11 **Get you** out of the way, turn aside out of the path, cause the Holy One of Israel to cease from before us.*

58. (GB) departed = (KJB) on his way

*(Geneva) Jeremiah 4:7 The lyon is come vp from his denne, and the destroyer of the Gentiles is **departed**, and gone forth of his place to lay thy land waste, and thy cities shalbe destroyed without an inhabitant.*

*(KJB) Jeremiah 4:7 The lion is come up from his thicket, and the destroyer of the Gentiles is **on his way**; he is gone forth from his place to make thy land desolate; and thy cities shall be laid waste, without an inhabitant.*

59. (GB) departed = (KJB) fled

*(Geneva) Jeremiah 4:25 I behelde, and loe, there was no man, and all the birdes of the heauen were **departed**.*

*(KJB) Jeremiah 4:25 I beheld, and, lo, there was no man, and all the birds of the heavens were **fled**.*

60. (GB) departed = (KJB) revolted

*(Geneva) Jeremiah 5:23 But this people hath an vnfaithfull and rebellious heart: they are **departed** and gone.*

*(KJB) Jeremiah 5:23 But this people hath a revolting and a rebellious heart; they are **revolted** and gone.*

61. (GB) depart = (KJB) pass away

*(Geneva) Jeremiah 8:13 I wil surely consume them, sayth the Lord: there shalbe no grapes on the vine, nor figges on the figtree, and the leafe shall fade, and the things that I haue giuen them, shal **depart** from them.*

*(KJB) Jeremiah 8:13 I will surely consume them, saith the LORD: there shall be no grapes on the vine, nor figs on the fig tree, and the leaf shall fade; and the things that I have given them shall **pass away** from them.*

62. (GB) depart = (KJB) go far off

*(Geneva) Ezekiel 8:6 He said furthermore vnto me, Sonne of ma, seest thou not what they doe? euen the great abominations that the house of Israel committeth here to cause me to **depart** from my Sanctuarie? but yet turne thee and thou shalt see greater abominations.*

*(KJB) Ezekiel 8:6 He said furthermore unto me, Son of man, seest thou what they do? even the great abominations that the house of Israel committeth here, that I should **go far off** from my sanctuary? but turn thee yet again, and thou shalt see greater abominations.*

63. (GB) Depart = (KJB) Get

*(Geneva) Ezekiel 11:15 Sonne of man, thy brethren, euen thy brethren, the men of thy kindred, & all the house of Israel, wholy are they vnto whome the inhabitants of Ierusalem haue said, **Depart** ye farre from the Lord: for the lande is giuen vs in possession.*

*(KJB) Ezekiel 11:15 Son of man, thy brethren, even thy brethren, the men of thy kindred, and all the house of Israel wholly, are they unto whom the inhabitants of Jerusalem have said, **Get** you far from the LORD: unto us is this land given in possession.*

64. (GB) departed = (KJB) estranged

*(Geneva) Ezekiel 14:5 That I may take the house of Israel in their owne heart, because they are all **departed** from me through their idoles.*

(KJB) Ezekiel 14:5 *That I may take the house of Israel in their own heart, because they are all* **estranged** *from me through their idols.*

65. (GB) departeth = (KJB) separateth himself

(Geneva) Ezekiel 14:7 *For euery one of the house of Israel, or of the stranger that soiourneth in Israel, which* **departeth** *from mee, and setteth vp his idoles in his heart, and putteth the stumbling blocke of his iniquitie before his face, and commeth to a Proverbs ophet, for to inquire of him for me, I the Lord will answere him for my selfe,*

(KJB) Ezekiel 14:7 *For every one of the house of Israel, or of the stranger that sojourneth in Israel, which* **separateth himself** *from me, and setteth up his idols in his heart, and putteth the stumblingblock of his iniquity before his face, and cometh to a prophet to inquire of him concerning me; I the LORD will answer him by myself:*

66. (GB) departed = (KJB) alienated

(Geneva) Ezekiel 23:17 *Nowe when the Babylonians came to her into the bed of loue, they defiled her with their fornication, and she was polluted with them, and her lust* **departed** *from them.*

(KJB) Ezekiel 23:17 *And the Babylonians came to her into the bed of love, and they defiled her with their whoredom, and she was polluted with them, and her mind was* **alienated** *from them.*

67. (GB) departed = (KJB) gone down

(Geneva) Ezekiel 31:12 *And the strangers haue destroyed him, euen the terrible nations, and they haue left him vpon the mountaines, and in all the valleis his branches are fallen, and his boughes are broken by all the riuers of the land: and all the people of the earth are* **departed** *from his shadowe, and haue forsaken him.*

(KJB) Ezekiel 31:12 *And strangers, the terrible of the nations, have cut him off, and have left him: upon the mountains and in all the valleys his branches are fallen, and his boughs are broken by all the rivers of the land; and all the people of the earth are* **gone down** *from his shadow, and have left him.*

68. (GB) depart = (KJB) pass

(Geneva) Zechariah 3:4 *And he answered and spake vnto those that stoode before him, saying, Take away the filthie garments from*

him. And vnto him hee saide, Behold, I haue caused thine iniquitie to **depart** *from thee, & I wil clothe thee with change of raiment.*

(KJB) Zechariah 3:4 *And he answered and spake unto those that stood before him, saying, Take away the filthy garments from him. And unto him he said, Behold, I have caused thine iniquity to* **pass** *from thee, and I will clothe thee with change of raiment..*

69. (GB) departed = (KJB) went

(Geneva) Matthew 8:32 *And he said vnto them, Go. So they went out and* **departed** *into the heard of swine: and beholde, the whole heard of swine ranne headlong into the sea, and died in the water.*

(KJB) Matthew 8:32 *And he said unto them, Go. And when they were come out, they* **went** *into the herd of swine: and, behold, the whole herd of swine ran violently down a steep place into the sea, and perished in the waters.*

70. (GB) departed = (KJB) withdrew himself from

(Geneva) Matthew 12:15 *But whe Iesus knew it, he* **departed** *thece, & great multitudes folowed him, & he healed the al,*

(KJB) Matthew 12:15 *But when Jesus knew it, he* **withdrew himself from** *thence: and great multitudes followed him, and he healed them all;*

71. (GB) departeth = (KJB) goeth

(Geneva) Matthew 13:44 *Againe, the kingdom of heauen is like vnto a treasure hid in ye field, which when a man hath found, he hideth it, & for ioy thereof* **departeth** *& selleth all yt he hath, and buieth that field.*

(KJB) Matthew 13:44 *Again, the kingdom of heaven is like unto treasure hid in a field; the which when a man hath found, he hideth, and for joy thereof* **goeth** *and selleth all that he hath, and buyeth that field.*

72. (GB) depart = (KJB) send…away

(Geneva) Matthew 15:32 *Then Iesus called his disciples vnto him, and said, I haue compassion on this multitude, because they haue continued with mee already three dayes, & haue nothing to eate: and I wil not let them* **depart** *fasting, least they faint in the way.*

*(KJB) Matthew 15:32 Then Jesus called his disciples unto him, and said, I have compassion on the multitude, because they continue with me now three days, and have nothing to eat: and I will not **send** them **away** fasting, lest they faint in the way.*

73. (GB) departing = (KJB) decease

*(Geneva) Luke 9:31 Which appeared in glory, and tolde of his **departing**, which he shoulde accomplish at Hierusalem.*

*(KJB) Luke 9:31 Who appeared in glory, and spake of his **decease** which he should accomplish at Jerusalem.*

74. (GB) departed = (KJB) parted

*(Geneva) Luke 24:51 And it came to passe, that as he blessed them, he **departed** from them, and was caried vp into heauen.*

*(KJB) Luke 24:51 And it came to pass, while he blessed them, he was **parted** from them, and carried up into heaven.*

75. (GB) departed = (KJB) dismissed

*(Geneva) Acts 15:30 Nowe when they were **departed**, they came to Antiochia, and after that they had assembled the multitude, they deliuered the Epistle.*

*(KJB) Acts 15:30 So when they were **dismissed**, they came to Antioch: and when they had gathered the multitude together, they delivered the epistle:*

76. (GB) departed = (KJB) gotten

*(Geneva) Acts 21:1 And as we launched forth, and were **departed** from them, we came with a straight course vnto Coos, and the day following vnto the Rhodes, and from thence vnto Patara.*

*(KJB) Acts 21:1 And it came to pass, that after we were **gotten** from them, and had launched, we came with a straight course unto Coos, and the day following unto Rhodes, and from thence unto Patara:*

77. (GB) departing = (KJB) falling away

*(Geneva) 2 Thessalonians 2:3 Let no man deceiue you by any meanes: for that day shall not come, except there come a **departing** first, and that that man of sinne be disclosed, euen the sonne of perdition,*

*(KJB) 2 Thessalonians 2:3 Let no man deceive you by any means: for that day shall not come, except there come a **falling away** first, and that man of sin be revealed, the son of perdition;*

78. (GB) departing = (KJB) decease

*(Geneva) 2 Peter1:15 I will endeuour therefore alwayes, that ye also may be able to haue remembrance of these things after my **departing**.*

*(KJB) 2 Peter 1:15 Moreover I will endeavour that ye may be able after my **decease** to have these things always in remembrance.*

The magnitude of the significance of this study cannot be overstated. This one word comparison of *depart* reveals the depth of word usage found in the King James Bible in the early 1600s versus the best known of its predecessors from only forty years earlier. Again, the differences do not reflect a problem with the pre-King James versions; the differences reflect what happens when a living language finally reaches its zenith during the publication of the King James Bible. Interestingly, the grammar was at its peak during this time, but standardized spelling did not take place until the mid 1700s, but that is another study in itself.

Index

Scripture Index